Everything you need to know,
before you need to know it

The Customer Relationship Management

Survival Guide

Dick Lee

The sequel to the category best-seller,
The Sales Automation Survival Guide.

The Customer Relationship Marketing Survival Guide—Everything you need to know, before you need to know it

Lee, Richard A.
        The Customer Relationship Marketing Survival Guide

ISBN 0-9673757-3-8
Library of Congress Catalog
Card Number 00 132423
1. Customer Relationship Management
2. Sales Force Automation   3. Marketing   4. Selling

Printed in the United States of America
$29.00 U.S.

Published by HYM Press, St. Paul, MN
info@h-ym.com - www.h-ym.com

Everything you need to know,
before you need to know it

The Customer Relationship Management
Survival Guide

Table of Contents

V. Sidebars

VI. Other Stuff

Acknowledgments

"Until you write a book, you have no idea how important acknowledgments are. That's because, by the time you finish, your family and friends are half-ready to either kill you or write you off as a babbling idiot who writes copy out loud at the dinner table…the movies…wherever. Never mind this pap about "patience," "support" and "love and understanding." They're ready to do terrible things to you! And that goes for your dear professional colleagues as well. Those who spent the entire time you were writing just waiting by the phone for your call. 'Mind reading this section over again, good buddy?'"

That's what I said after writing *The Sales Automation Survival Guide*. Since then, I've replayed this scenario with *The Customer Relationship Management Planning Guide,* now this. How many ways can you spell D-O-G-H-O-U-S-E ?

Seriously, you can't write one book without ending up indebted to a lot of people. And a second and a third? I need to deliver as many "thank yous" as Santa delivers presents. But I'm older than Santa, and I don't have her energy. So forgive me for just saying a big, blanket "thank you"—to all my clients, my professional colleagues, my friends and my imaginary staff who listen to me when I get tired of talking to myself. Thanks again!

But I have to get much more specific than that on two accounts. First, my appreciation to my very real support staff—Kathie Anderson, my favorite editor, who tames my verbal violence and makes sure the serious side of this book is always visible through the sarcasm; prepress production manager Kristine Anderson (not a sister act); and cover designer Jody Majeres. Then, and most important of all, more than thanks to my very patient and understanding family. My wife, Kathryne Sanders, who's developed "knitter's elbow" waiting for me to have a free weekend—and our eight year-old, Gus, who at school draws crayon pictures of me with captions like, "Dad works all the time." Whoops—guess I better go pick up the football and throw him a few. Then kick the soccer ball. Then go ice fishing. Before he starts writing too. Then we'll never see each other.

Dick Lee
dlee@h-ym.com

Customer Relationship Management

Implementing customer-centric business strategies,
which drives redesigning of functional activities,
which demands re-engineering of work processes,
which is supported, *not driven,* by CRM technology.

Introduction

The road to hell is paved with good intentions.
So too the road to CRM.

Today, no marketing or technology topic, aside from the Internet, is creating more of a stir than "customer relationship management"—now ubiquitously called "CRM." And no wonder why. Customers are taking over the buyer-seller relationship—and that's not just a lot of marketing hype. Listen to the view from the *technology* side of business.

> The new age of customer-centric computing moves the focus from platforms to people; and very specifically to the new drivers of change in the 21st century: customers.[1]

No marketer or traditional customer advocate could say it better.

CRM is the force that moves customers to the center of our business circle. And that's why it's so hot. Consider this. The

---

[1] "The Customer Really is King," Bob Evans, senior editor, *Information Week,* March 1999.

---

research firm, META Group, projects the market for just CRM tools will grow from a whopping $4.7 billion in 2001 to an almost inconceivable $10 billion in 2003. And Anderson Consulting projects that 50% of U.S. businesses will be organized around customer types by year 2002—up from only 18% in 1999. Overly optimistic? The Anderson numbers are—but discount them by 50% and that's still eye-popping.

But not only is CRM white hot, it's confusing. Perhaps no topic, including the Internet, is causing more confusion. Some see CRM as the new miracle drug that can cure sales and marketing inefficiency, which they perceive as the last corporate sinkhole. For others, especially those who jumped first, CRM has proved to be a relatively untested drug that was rushed to market before discovery of its powerful side effects, which can kill the patient. Yet others view CRM as a method of fundamentally changing human behavior. And this view is countered by the popular perception that CRM is a software commodity, which is purchased and distributed to employees much like a new word processor. Confusion? No kidding. But throughout this book I'll reconcile these conflicting views and totally trash the concept of CRM as "software." And there's more. Another point of confusion is the term itself, "CRM." What does it really mean? In rapid succession, CRM has broken through its original "sales force automation" boundaries to include first customer service, then marketing, then information technology (IT). Now it's infiltrating such powerful principalities as financial services, manufacturing, logistics and purchasing—places where it's either unwelcome or subject to being shot on sight. And finally, it's reaching its ultimate destination—the executive suite and the boardroom.

But that's where it's going, not what it is. So what is it?

Here are just some of the mixed bag of CRM definitions being batted around, ranging from the sublime to the ridiculous.

CRM n. 1: a customer-focused approach to business. 2: work flow and information flow designed around the needs of the customer first, and the internal needs of the enterprise second. 3: customer information management capability at the point of customer contact. 4: linking all customer-related information in the enterprise into one information system, focused at the point of customer contact. 5: introduction of information-based process management to sales and marketing. 6: the combination of sales, service and marketing automation software. 7: web-based, thin client software that moves customer information over the Internet. 8: e.*. 9: *.com. 10: new age database marketing. Huh?

And truth be told, none of these common descriptions, good or bad, express the totality of CRM. But add up the first half, and you pretty much get the picture. Especially if you ignore the last half. And we'll drill down lots more as we go, at least touching on every facet of CRM. Sound interesting to you?

Having said all that, let me add what this book is *not* about. This book is not about being a shill for CRM and the CRM industry. Yeah, CRM is hot and cool and trendy. And it's still in its early adolescence, with years more explosive growth ahead. But CRM is an adolescent with a troubled past—and present—and potentially a troubled future.

You need to know about this, too. From the get-go, CRM promises huge gains in customer lifetime value as well as greatly diminished customer churn. It also promises to cure the inherent inefficiency of the sales process or the lack of sales process. And it even promises to harness the power of the Internet. Hey, if CRM can help us more effectively acquire and manage contact-level customer information, help us use that information to cash in on more customer development opportunities, keep our customers around longer so we don't have to spend lots on marketing to replace them, and even encourage more productivity from field sales representatives (those folks who deserve to be burned at the stake for filling the trunks of their company cars with golf clubs, fishing tackle and other gear to play with while everyone else is working)—not to mention bring the Internet to heel—if CRM can accomplish all this, how can we go wrong?

Easy.

Depending on whose numbers you use, between 60% and 80% of CRM implementations fail to deliver on their core promises, or anything close. And somewhere between 30% and 50% are abject failures. According to Jim Dickie of Denver-based Insight Technology Group, the unofficial (but I believe accurate) CRM industry pollster, only 31% of CRM implementations are generating meaningful ROI as we head into year 2000. That's how easily CRM can go awry. Sure we're making some progress. But the numbers are improving at a snail's pace.

From a pavement-level perspective, CRM usually produces more pain than gain. And while there's plenty of blame to spread around for CRM's tendency to burn implementers, nothing leads to more pain than treating CRM as a software system—a mistake that occurs in a majority of first-time CRM implementations. And recurs in those organizations immune to learning from past experience.

Here's the drill. Some speed-is-life senior executive reads a few ads and then tells some poor subordinate to buy "this brand" of highly-advertised CRM software. So the subordinate buys a gazillion dollars of some hoity-toity system with more ornaments than a Christmas tree. Then the software company jury-rigs the system so it looks like it would work for the buyer's company. Next the company deploys this CRM software system to the poor bastards on the receiving end—the nameless, faceless folks who deal with customers—who roundly reject it and won't use it. Swell.

Think I'm exaggerating?

Unfortunately, I'm not. And what happens next? Mr. Speed I. Life blames his failure to follow any form of due diligence implementing CRM on this suddenly "lousy" software—or on the hapless souls on the receiving end of this folly. Then he either replaces the software with a new set of bells and whistles or starts replacing the salespeople who won't use this stuff. Sort of like shooting yourself in the foot with a pistol, then picking up a machine gun to do it right.

That's why we cannot repeat to ourselves too often:

CRM is not software.

Instead, CRM is the aggregation of: 1) *customer-centric strategies;* 2) which drive new functional activity not only for sales, marketing and service, but often back-office functions such as accounting, production scheduling and shipping; 3) which demand *re-engineered work processes* for everyone affected; 4) which require *technology support* to implement.

Four levels of impact. And when you roll 'em all up, you've got enough change going on to tear even a solid company from its moorings. Because organizations take CRM so lightly, the pain that inevitably accompanies any such organizational and cultural shift of this magnitude comes as a shock. So much so that even the first pangs stop some CRM projects dead in their tracks. "No one told us this was going to happen." "Yeah, it's important, but we can't afford to tick off so and so." "You're not messing with any of my direct reports." And, "Hey, why torture ourselves over a piece of software?" Good question, if that's all CRM is.

And you can imagine what hits the fan when an executive VP in charge of all information technology discovers that some less-than-executive VP of sales and marketing is running a competitive information system using mail-order laptops and some strange hybrid of process management and database software! Or when the executive VP of operations discovers that someone's trying to pirate his customer service department and move them to the front office, where they'll report in through marketing. Or when some division president or other discovers that her reports in district management are being asked to have their district salespeople pipe volumes of district-level customer information back to some John or Jane Doe marketing analyst at corporate. Like running a manure spreader with the wind at your back.

Remember those CRM failure rates quoted just a few paragraphs back? Those represent only the CRM implementations that get off the drawing board. From what I've experienced wading through the wreckage left by failed or partially installed, never-finished projects, we're at the midpoint of that range or higher—and if we include CRM initiatives that die or go on permanent hold during the preliminary discussion stage, that percentage would rise higher yet.

Obviously, there's a problem. The temptation of tremendous gains in sales and marketing productivity is hanging out there like the proverbial carrot—and most who reach for those gains are getting whacked with the proverbial stick.

Why?

Answering the "why" question for potential victims was the primary reason for writing this book. We'll take a close look at what's behind CRM failures to make sure you're forewarned and forearmed.

Whether you're in sales, marketing, customer service, information technology, operations or corporate management, reading this book should greatly increase the odds that you'll be ready to do your part in the complex process of implementing CRM in your organization. And the book won't just look at potential problems. We're going to focus on the possibilities as well. After all, we don't want to discourage you from doing CRM. Quite the contrary. We want to keep your feet out of buckets of CRM stuff so you'll do CRM successfully. That way you'll reap all the benefits CRM offers today—and better yet, you'll be perfectly positioned to reap a much bigger harvest tomorrow, as CRM matures. And that "tomorrow" is not far away.

For example, while technology limitations, such as the difficulty in getting different databases to communicate with each other, still hinder CRM's progression beyond the boundaries of sales, marketing and sometimes customer service, some linkages between CRM and back-office operations and financial systems are already in place, and more are on the way. And with the advent of Microsoft's SQL Server 7.0 database, a model of open architecture that's already the *de facto* standard for CRM databases and becoming widely used in the back office, these limitations are history, at least they will be soon.

The net of increased integration will be real enterprise CRM (that's more than hot air and advertising claims)—where CRM systems will extend from the point of customer contact right into the bowels of corporate information systems, encompassing every piece of information pertaining to each individual customer. One and only one record for each customer, how about that? No duplicate data kept anywhere! You're about to get a sneak preview of where the CRM phenomenon is headed, and where you just might want to head yourself.

Four quick notes before we start (which by definition, isn't quick). First, I have a responsibility to my clients not to let competitors know what they're up to—not to mention confidentiality contracts that land me in hot water if I do blab. So I don't. And other consultants who've shared their stories with me share that same responsibility. Consequently, I've disguised all specific client references to discourage guessing. So don't guess. You'll be wrong.

Second, about my seeming skew toward salespeople at various points in the book. I'm not an apologist for the sales profession. In fact, I take a dim view of the profession's persistent resistance to process improvement, technology and almost any other form of change. Yet, from the sales side of the fence, I also understand how much of sales' "negative behavior" is giving back what they get. I also know that CRM is virtually impossible to implement in an environment where attitudes such as "getting back at sales" or "teaching sales a lesson" or "bringing sales to heel" are mixed in with CRM.

Before implementing CRM, we all need to swallow hard and exorcise whatever rancor we hold toward any CRM participants. And if we have a hard time doing so with regard to sales, try looking in the mirror and asking why we're not jumping at the opportunity to earn their money and enjoy goofing off on the job. Heck, virtually every one of my clients asks me for help finding good salespeople. There's a job waiting for you out there—if you enjoy burnout, love rejection and thrive on living with uncertainty. Not to mention the enjoyment of being dumped on by everyone who envies your pay and your "freedom"—but doesn't have a clue about the price you pay, nor a willingness to pay it if they did. And let's not ignore the threat of losing your job to e-commerce—although the dire predictions of the imminent demise of the sales profession are inane, to be generous.

Think I'm pushing a point too far? Take it from another source. Here's what Eugene Johnson, marketing professor and co-author of the recent study "Attitudes of College Students Towards Selling" has to say.

> They [college students] believe there is money to be made in sales, but they often don't want to do the necessary things to make that money.[2]

Amen.

Third, there's the e.gagme.com factor. As you read merrily along, you may wonder why this book doesn't have a greater

---

[2] Andy Cohen, "Sales Strikes Out on Campus," *Sales and Marketing Management*, November 1997.

focus on e-commerce and the Internet. Well, let me assure you that I do believe strongly in the power of both. In fact, a successful e-commerce venture is why yours truly can afford taking time to write books. And after I write them, a little book store named amazon.com sells more of them than all other retail outlets combined. Which is not only slicker than you know what, but it also cuts out some very greedy middlemen. And if that doesn't convince you, I'm currently deep in strategic planning with a client for a series of new, knock-your-socks-off web ventures. So I do love the Internet and web-based stuff—when used in appropriate contexts.

However, the fact that I love it and love what it's done for me doesn't make me lose sight of one fundamental fact: CRM ain't e.com. And I'm sick of having a bunch of yahoos (not the portal and search engine folks) trying to ram all this e.crap down everyone's throats. Of course e-commerce and the Internet overall will play vitally important roles in CRM—but they don't always now, and they'll never be the whole ball of wax. E-commerce (pardon me, e-commerce) is among the many choices we have for selling stuff. The Internet (and extranets) is among the many choices we have for communicating stuff. But both can be the wrong choices today. And both could be the wrong choices for many customers in the future—especially when we try to use them to the exclusion of traditional channels.

And fourth, about the tenor of the book. You've had just a taste of my sarcasm. I assure you, it will only get worse. I considered toning it down. But every time that thought arose, so did the image of a delicious quote from Freud, which I saw posted outside a client's office door.

Insanity.
Doing the same thing over and over again, but expecting a different outcome.

That's an apt description of CRM today. We keep trying. Most of us keep failing. And we keep on making the same damn mistakes, over and over again. And to compound the problem, we keep losing our focus on what CRM is...and is not. Which further fuels the failure rate.

The time has passed for a polite tome about this or that aspect of CRM. It's time to start getting in people's faces about this stuff. Which is why I take every opportunity to disabuse the notion that CRM is only software, the concept that CRM is merely a process improvement tool and other equally off-base (and usually self-serving) thinking.

Besides, on a personal level, it's getting really hard to see companies get burned—only to have more leapfrog over them, right into the fires of CRM hell. Hey, I love this stuff too much—and hate to see so many getting hurt by it. So please forgive a periodic acid tongue—and some very tough defending of CRM principles.

I. Understanding CRM

History

No doubt about it—the sales and marketing landscape is changing right before our very eyes. And CRM is playing a big role. But where the heck are sales and marketing really headed? What's CRM technology got to do with it? And should CRM systems be leading sales and marketing or the other way around?

Brain teasers. Too bad a few CRM software sellers think they're no brainers. Hey, accept as gospel the preachings from the software pulpit and here's what to expect. "Technology's gonna take over sales and marketing. Marketing's moving to the Net. Sales? Who needs 'em. Hey, before long the Net and e-commerce (of course guided by CRM software) will rule." Simple.

Not simple, simplistic. This "technology rules" stuff is software industry sales pitch—with a choir of IT-first folks singing harmony. Nothing about CRM is simple. We're talking four interdependent levels of impact working in sequence. You might call it a ripple effect. When new relationship marketing strategies are put into play, they trigger new functional activities; which trigger new work processes, steps and tasks; which trigger needs for technology support. Just like dropping a stone in the water and sending out concentric circles of waves.

But bye the bye, have you ever seen the reverse ripple effect—reversing the wave action so the stone pops back out? Dumb question, eh? But if it's so dumb, why do so many CRM jockeys start with technology, which is then supposed to change processes, which are somehow supposed to drive functional activities, which are ultimately supposed to coalesce into coherent strategies? Gulp. Guess we know now why technology-driven CRM projects do tend to crash and burn. No matter how hard you try, that darn stone never seems to pop back out of the water.

This "technology rules" stuff is software industry sales pitch—with a choir of IT-first folks singing harmony.

So let's skip "simple" and get serious about this stuff.

Sales and marketing are indeed in the midst of some heavy changes. And it's darned easy to mistake what's going on. In fact, some changes are almost opposite what they appear to be at first glance. For example, what's commonly mistaken for a technology *revolution* driving sales and marketing changes is really an *evolutionary* response to unmet sales and marketing needs—needs that some in sales and marketing have been sitting around and waiting 20 years to see met.

The "CRM Ripple Effect"

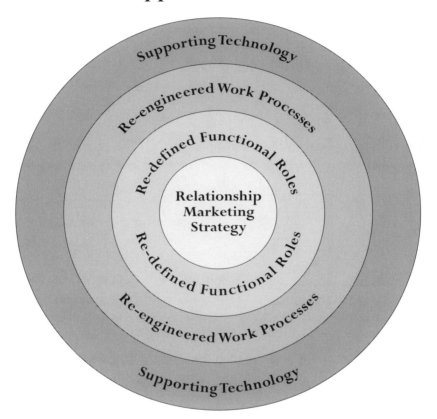

Effective CRM development follows a concentric pattern—
starting with relationship strategies and working outward.

Let's remember that. CRM technology is an evolutionary response to environmental changes. If we ignore how CRM as a whole came about, and ignore how sales and marketing and CRM technology got where they are, we won't *get it* about where they're going. And if we continue to not get it, CRM will go right on disappointing lots of folks who try to use it without understanding what it is.

So let's rewind a bit—actually, all the way back to the 1950s. See what was going on with marketing and sales. Yeah, I know history is boring. But so is continuing to screw up CRM. So let's grit our teeth for five minutes so we can figure out where we are, and why.

We're going that far back because that's when the whole concept of customer relationships went into the tank, and our merchant- and sales-driven economy ended. *Finis.* At least for then. And contrary to popular perception, television didn't end it. Customers did. Customers had money, they had confidence and they had enough of *doing without* because of the war. So they started spending their brains out—business and consumer customers alike. And the demand curve kept shooting higher and the supply curve couldn't keep up.

> **History is boring. But so is continuing to screw up CRM.**

What did customers want from marketing and sales back then? Pizzazz. Sizzle. Excitement over the prospect of owning this product or that. And that's what marketing delivered—on television, radio, billboards, in a whole new category of advertising-driven business publications. Amazing what you can get printed editorially in some pubs by placing a full-page, four-color ad. And it was "one-fits-all" for products, for marketing messages, everything. And it was so darned easy. Who needed to work for business?

What about sales? Willy Loman[3] time. Mass marketing swiped a big chunk of sales' role. Nobody loves a loser, so respect for the sales profession went down like a sky diver without a parachute. Cooperation between sales and marketing? Non-existent. They had virtually nothing to do with each other. And if Einstein had been a nerd instead of a physicist,

---

[3] Willy Loman is the lead character in Arthur Miller's classic drama, *Death of a Salesman.*

and CRM technology (and hence CRM) was possible back then, any need for it? Not a chance. Points out that CRM is dependent on the market environment—in other words, dependent on customers. That's peculiar. Not the way many think of CRM. "Hey, we're out to manage customers." Too bad you're not back in the fifties, fellow.

That's the way things stayed for some 30 years. So let's fast forward to the early 1980s. That's when customers started smartening up to what they'd let happen—mass production, mass marketing, whatever sellers wanted.

What changed customers? Again, the economy. After three decades of demand curve over supply curve, the two curves started reversing position. Not in every business sector. But especially in expensive stuff that computers helped us design better and make faster. Customers started seeing more options and more opportunity to have things their way. So they started demanding more. More individual attention. More responsiveness. More customization. Stuff that CRM and CRM technology helps us provide.

So what did marketing do? Nothing. Just kept right on mass advertising. Why quit when you're on a roll?

> **As a sop to the whiners complaining about wasting bucks on broad media coverage, marketers invented "target marketing"— which was nothing more than shriveled up mass marketing.**

Besides, individual customer contact was sales stuff. Beneath marketing. But as a sop to the whiners complaining about wasting bucks on broad media coverage, marketers invented "target marketing"—which was nothing more than shriveled up mass marketing. Did the trick, though.

Got everyone complaining about getting "too much mass marketing" off their backs. Everyone except for a few of us newfangled, "relationship marketers" who wanted to customize marketing, pay attention to individual customers, customize products and services to suit the smallest possible universe, even the universe of one. What planet were we on?

Hey, some really good strategies emerged from this fledgling relationship marketing movement, back in the 1980s. A few even got put into play. But most died in the thinking stage. Lack of CRM-type technology to pull it off. No tools, no technology, no dice.

But early relationship marketers did make enough headway to start splitting marketing into two bodies, each going in different directions. One "body" was Jesse "The Body" Ventura size and the other was of hangnail proportions—but the whole body would soon feel this nail tearing away.

> **Early relationship marketers did make enough headway to start splitting marketing into two bodies, each going in different directions.**

And sales? Sales started a comeback. Got more professional. Took more responsibility for understanding technical products. And sales really benefited from the supply/demand switch. The core marketing issue for many companies changed from getting the word out to getting the product in—into more crowded distribution, onto more crowded store shelves, in through more selective business and industrial buyers. "Getting the word out" was a job for media. "Getting the product in" was a job for sales. So sales got more important. Got paid more. But respect? Still in Willy Loman-land, except in a select few companies—the likes of 3M, IBM, Xerox.

Cooperation between sales and marketing? The idea actually crept into a few heads. Hey, couldn't afford expensive sales people wasting valuable time cold calling. Get marketing to drum up some sales leads. Course, marketing didn't want to muck up their ads with unseemly coupons and big, bold 800 numbers. Ugh. But inconspicuous "reader service" numbers that readers could circle on bingo cards to request more information were okay. So marketing generated a gazillion bingo card inquiries—raw inquiries, mostly from tire kickers—then piped them to sales. Sales flushed them down the toilet. What teamwork.

But a few of us actually tried stepping between the two. We set up third-party inquiry management systems that tele-qualified sales inquiries, distributed only qualified sales leads, promptly fulfilled serious requests for product and company information, monitored follow-up to make sure sales showed up, measured both sales and media outcomes and established some surprisingly sophisticated work process stuff—and computer-managed the whole shebang. But it was pretty manual and pretty hard. Not exactly automation. Not exactly very profitable, either, when we had to spend $35,000 for a 75MB hard drive. And then there was the shooting that started every time we "stepped between."

Would CRM fly in this environment? Hey, you could see it trying. And if enough tools and technology had been available, it might have gotten off the ground—back in the early 1980s.

Now let's fast forward to the mid 1990s—but with a finger on the "pause" button—'85, '86, '87, '88, PAUSE. What happened then? Database marketing technology started making its way to the desktop. And some folks started managing databases instead of shoveling direct mail down the chute. Produced "targeted direct mail." So mass mailings became shriveled up mass mailings. Did that bring CRM any closer? If anything, it pushed CRM further away.

These database denizens proclaimed their craft the future of all marketing. "We're going to do away with mass advertising." By sending mass mailings. Even shriveled up ones. Yeah, right. What no one but a few relationship marketers scattered around seemed to realize was that database marketing is promotional talking. Relationship marketing—and CRM—are about listening, and about customer communication that doesn't have to be promotional because it responds to customer interests and issues. Not much overlap. But lots of confusion between database marketing and relationship marketing—for awhile. More on that later.

Let's fast forward again—'89, '90, '91, '92, '93, PAUSE. In 1993, Don Peppers' and Martha Rogers' landmark book, *The One to One Future: Building Relationships One Customer at a Time*[4] came out swinging at mass marketing. Cleared up some of the confusion caused by database marketing, too. And started a tug of war with the database crowd over which was really the "new marketing"—database or one-to-one (relationship marketing). Stimulated lots of relationship marketing thinking, too. But same outcomes as 15 years ago when relationship marketing emerged. No tools, no technology, no dice. However, the frustration from trying to go one-to-one did hasten the by now very belated emergence of CRM technology. That's our next stop.

Fast forward one more time—'94, '95, '96, PAUSE. Finally, a little help from technology. Sales force automation (SFA) stumbled out of the shadows and into the limelight. Actually, SFA first made more than a token appearance in the late 1980s, but most of the early stuff was "contact management" for individual sales people. Helped some. But left individual sales people isolated—islands unto themselves. Then connectivity through "synchronizing" data within user groups appeared. Then came client-server networking. Then synchronization and networking got reliable enough for prime time—which produced an explosion of user interest in SFA that hit in 1996 and 1997.

---

[4] *The One to One Future*, Don Peppers and Martha Rogers, Ph.D., Doubleday, 1994.

Nirvana? Nope. Unfortunately, SFA was pretty much a dud. It generated more software sales than anything else. Why? Because it isolated sales *departments*, rather than integrating them with marketing or customer service. SFA also lacked the open architecture required to access back-office data—although in fairness, integrating data from different systems, any systems, was still pretty dicey. But SFA's big failing was being a tactical tool trying to fill a strategic need. Rather than help us implement new relationship marketing strategies, SFA helped us do things the old way faster. Automating cow paths. Sure it helped us tinker around with work processes, and it might have satisfied user needs back in the early 1980s, but it was way too little way too late.

> **Unfortunately, SFA was pretty much a dud.**

So let's end this history stuff and fast forward to the present—and see what's up today, in year 2000. The economy is booming. But no matter how hard it booms, we've still got more supply capacity than demand. Sure we have spot shortages—computer chips, drywall, caviar—but we've gotten too good at making most stuff to run out, and customers know it. And then we have the Internet—which doesn't change everything, but does change a lot. It's a new communication channel where we can leave information for customers to come and get—when they want. It's a distribution channel where customers can come and buy stuff—when they want. And for customers, it's an alternative to wading through glitzy advertising to find out about stuff—and an alternative to putting up with "insistence and persistence" sales people who can't answer a question without giving a sales pitch.

Where are customers' heads? Hey, take all the changes that started in the early '80s and ratchet them up ten points. They want even more individual attention, even more responsiveness and much more customization. Stuff that CRM is meant to provide.

They're also insisting that we approach them as one company—rather than piling up six sales reps in their lobby, one from each division, all seeing the same buyer. And they want everyone dealing with them to know what's going on. None of this, "I'll have to check with your sales rep." They're also building long-term supplier relationships based on trust and mutual respect. Hey, CRM can help deliver lots of stuff they want. Oh, and they've got their heads up on the Net. Lets them do what they want, when they want, without anyone ragging on them to buy this or that. Except for yo-yos who record everyone who visits their site, then bug the you-know-what out of them, just like the old days.

So what is marketing doing about dealing with the "new customer." Mass marketing as always. At least mainstream marketing is. Trying to turn the Internet into a television channel, too. But mainstream marketing is only half the equation, now (well, maybe two-thirds). That "hangnail" regenerated itself into a living breathing body that's grown strong enough to tear away and live independently. Relationship marketing is coming of age—and now has some of the tools and technology it needs.

Relationship marketing is coming of age—and now has some of the tools and technology it needs.

But what about database marketing? Well, these folks tried to keep one foot in each camp. When the split widened—well, you get the picture. A few finally scurried back to mainstream marketing, but the majority tried to crowd onto the new territory that CRM—the new combination of relationship marketing strategies and CRM systems—started staking out in the late 1990s. They invented something called "marketing automation" so they wouldn't be left out. And some is new stuff, good stuff that helps initiate and build customer relationships through information management and analysis. But a lot of it is old, promotional database marketing in a new wrapper—straight out of the 1980s when marketing was all talk and little listening. Hard to disguise those "drek" mail packages—even if you dress 'em up as e-mail. Now I'm not talking about the "nurture marketing" or "drip marketing" style of customer contact pioneered by Jim Cecil.[5] Done right, that's powerful, relationship-building stuff. But the promotional stuff—including the stuff dressed up with phone personalization.

Cooperation between sales and marketing? Still no cooperation between mainstream marketers and sales. But the relationship side of marketing, get this, *likes* sales—and *respects* sales. In an increasing number of companies, relationship marketers and sales are learning to work together, gradually overcoming the "departmental divide."

And what about CRM technology? Where does that fit in? By melding sales, marketing and service information systems, CRM technology is the jackhammer breaking down the silos separating customer-facing functions. And by providing information exchange with back-office functions, it's even penetrating the "Berlin Wall" separating front office from back office. Hey, sales and accounting can sit in the same room without doing bodily harm to each other. Occasionally, anyway. But most importantly, by linking disparate functions CRM technology is finally evolving toward what relationship marketing needed a long time ago. Better late than never.

So now we're back where we started—asking "where the heck are sales and marketing really headed?" And "What's CRM technology really got to do with it?" And "Should CRM systems be leading sales and marketing or the other way around?"

Except we've already answered the questions. Just follow the trend lines. Sales and marketing started heading where they're headed 20 years ago. They'd be further along if CRM-type technology had arrived sooner, but they've been progressing

---

[5] You can find out more at *www.nurturemarketing.com*.

nonetheless. And now that technology has started catching up, sales and marketing, at least the relationship part, are about to start high-stepping into their future—together, arm in arm. Yup, sales and relationship marketing, following the trend lines, are melding into one integrated discipline. "Smarketing!"

In response to customer demands, we're about ready to start treating customer relationships as a continuum—not a linear series of interactions with one functional department after another. And that *will* change everything, especially sales and marketing. "Smarketing," the natural result of the continuous customer relationship, will realign corporate org charts, create new jobs, abolish old ones, change the profile of customer-facing personnel. Sure, traditional marketing will live

Sales and marketing started heading where they're headed 20 years ago.

on—for packaged goods and commodity marketing. So will good ol' "foot-in-the-back" selling—on car lots and carnival midways. But where buyers want genuine relationships with sellers—they'll happen. Even if that requires abolishing entire distribution channels, as may soon happen in the retail car biz. What customers want, customers get. And they want this.

And what about CRM technology's future role? We can see that also, from the past. CRM technology is the enabler—the indispensable tool for forming and maintaining the new genre of customer relationships. But it *won't* determine the nature of customer relationships. And neither will Internet technology. Customers will call those shots. CRM technology can make it all possible—as our window to customers and as the continuous information flow to support continuous relationships. But it can also make it all impossible, or at least very difficult, by failing to follow our customers' lead—and by failing to continue evolving to meet sales and marketing needs. CRM technology, or lack thereof, has held back sales and marketing before. It could do it again.

Impact Range of CRM vs. SFA

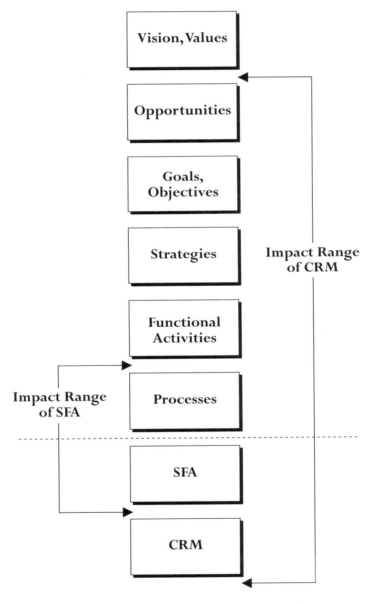

CRM is strategic, whereas SFA is tactical.

Technology

What better time to talk CRM technology than right after we finished bad-mouthing it half to death. But hey, we better keep some balance here, or I'll wind up in a cardboard box on a Software R Us shelf.

Seriously, among the lessons we've learned over the past 20 years is that implementing relationship marketing strategies without adequate technology support is an exercise in futility. The majority of the time, anyway. And over the last several years we've learned the futility of implementing CRM software without relationship marketing strategies. So we're stuck with each other. Strange bedfellows. Customer hand-holders and plastic pocket-liners. You hold my nose and I'll hold yours.

> **Among the lessons we've learned over the past 20 years is that implementing relationship marketing strategies without adequate technology support is an exercise in futility.**

Seriously again (well, at least I keep trying), some of my best friends are technologists. And I consult for several technology companies, too, so let's lighten up for a sentence or two.

CRM technology that works, does so on two levels. A high level where it dramatically affects enterprise information flow. And a lower level where it gives us new software tools to access and manage customer-related information—plus manage the often complex work processes required to carry out relationship marketing strategies. So where do you think the CRM industry has focused, on the higher level or lower level? Think small, and you'll get the right answer. That's right, CRM has a hard time being strategic, even within the friendly confines of information management!

But we were going to ignore that little problem and start at the top and work down.

Information flow

Introducing CRM challenges beliefs, customs and work processes that are deeply ingrained in most corporate cultures. For example:

CRM reverses customer data flow. Who would dare think of developing a corporate information system without basing it on management information needs? Remember, we used to call IT "MIS," as in "Management Information Systems." Well, the label has changed, but the philosophy hasn't, at least for much of the IT community. But anyone serious about CRM would put management information needs *second* to requirements for building successful customer relationships. You take care of them that pays the bills *first,* right?

CRM system development starts where customer information is gathered, then works back to the back office where accounting, manufacturing, etc., hang their hats—then relevant data goes back the other way. But that's heresy to many IT folks—because data flow supposedly *starts* in the back office, goes out, then comes back. And that's how IT systems are designed. But heresy or not, attempting to maintain traditional information system design parameters by working from "corporate out" has led to many expensive CRM failures—and even more stalled projects that can't move forward, because customer information flow can't fight the current.

Effective CRM systems decrease the total volume of customer information moving from point to point. Say what? How can adding a hefty information management component like CRM decrease data flow? Pretty simple, actually. The bulk of the data that customer relationship managers capture aids only the sales and service processes, with lesser amounts useful to marketing for developing relationship marketing initiatives in cooperation with sales and service. The smaller share of customer data that should go back to corporate—such as sales volume, sales pipeline projections, competitive intelligence, customer impressions of products and services, early warnings about shifts in buyer behavior, reasons why we're doing better with some customer groups than others, the impact of our advertising and promotion, new product and service opportunities—is extraordinarily valuable, but very low in volume. Extremely low compared to transferring gobs of statistical data that few ever look at or use.

CRM moves only *actionable* customer data up line, which doesn't require much information transportation. Then well-designed CRM systems force corporate data denizens to download data to them with a spoon, not a shovel. The net combined effect can reduce total data flow—substantially. Now I can hear some IT traditionalists screaming in the background, "What about data security? You can't leave data exposed in some sales and marketing system that runs on Windows." Yes you can folks. Backing up CRM data at the CRM server level (we'll explain that shortly) is hardly a big deal today. And Windows 2000 may actually be more stable than many flexibility-challenged back-office systems. So there.

But what about the Internet. Isn't the Net going to generate enormous volumes of data that spill into the company like water over Niagra Falls? Not if we're smart, it won't. As more and more communication with customers and the world at large migrates to the Internet, we'll have the opportunity to generate lots more raw data and dump it into giant data warehouses—where we'll stir it all up so we can cook up something good. But remember the old computer saying, "Garbage in, garbage out." Let someone else eat that stuff. If you focus on valuable, actionable data, you'll have a pipeline of new data to absorb—but it won't be a sewer pipe.

CRM inverts the traditional data pyramid. Traditionally, IT is the keeper of most data and the keeper of the only *official* data—including customer data.

At a conceptual level, most organizations conceive information management to be a high, corporate-level function and selling and servicing customers at a lower level. Accordingly, most corporate people hold a subconscious perception that concentrations of any type of organizational data, including customer data, innately belong in the corporate environment. CRM, carried beyond a simple sharing of contact information, directly challenges this presumption.

The charts on the following two pages show the change in information concentration that CRM can bring about. These charts have elicited many a gulp from first-time viewers. A couple of years ago, I met with a client from among the companies most responsible for the desktop revolution. His organization was attempting to establish a customer data warehouse at HQ—and failing. We'd discussed the problems they were experiencing, including the notion that data warehousing was the wrong solution. But I wasn't communicating my concerns in a meaningful way. So I showed him these charts. He put his head in his hands and blurted, "No wonder this isn't working."

Then, being the merciful type, I added, "You've reinvented IBM." In retrospect, he should have clocked me.

Corporate-centric customer data flow

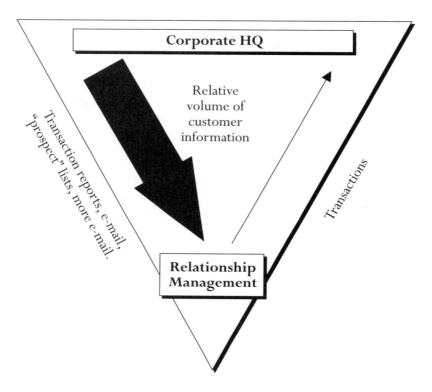

The traditional corporate-centric model
mostly pushes data at the field.

Customer-centric data flow

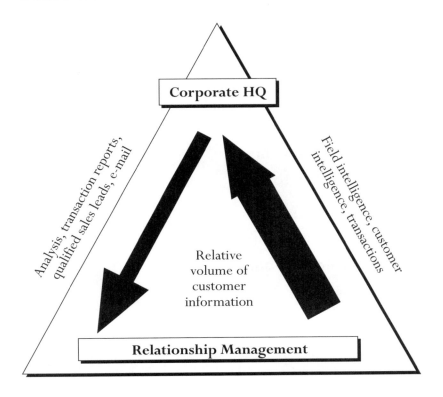

Customer-centric data flow is more balanced, with much more emphasis on uploading customer feedback and information.

In a CRM setting, relationship management needs come first. The principal users of CRM are relationship managers, primarily in sales and service. They already have full-time jobs, other than acquiring and managing data. Yet corporate can't take data gathering off their hands, because who else would gather data at the point of customer contact? Some data can be acquired through telemarketing, but not the most and not the best stuff. Relationship managers have to mine for that, which means they need extra hours in their day. Something has to give, and that something is the *administrative communication* required of relationship managers.

CRM must be designed to lighten the relationship managers' load—by making reporting faster and easier, by automating quote/proposal preparation and all manner of customer communication, by speeding up the process of obtaining product and service information, and by shortening the time required to communicate internally. And you know what? Typically, none of these *administrative* information exchanges are even considered when IT defines corporate information flow. Too insignificant. But ask even your best sales reps what percentage of their time is spent on these tasks. Expect the worst and you still may be stunned by how much time they spend off line and away from customers. Include reading corporate e-mail in the "time wasted" calculation and the numbers get outright scary.

> **Most organizations are unaccustomed to taking care of relationship management needs first and corporate management needs second.**

The sticking point here is that most organizations are unaccustomed to taking care of relationship management needs first and corporate management needs second. Being unprepared for this switch in priorities usually leads to assessing CRM needs in closed corporate meetings, with little or no contact-level input. In which case, the CRM they come up with inevitably places additional off-line responsibilities on sales and service, rather than lightening their load.

Among the most thoroughly depressing meetings I've ever attended was a milestone CRM project review meeting at the corporate offices of an international service marketer. Very telling was the fact that only IT people plus a token staff marketer were invited (I was not invited, but attended as someone's guest). No sales representation in sight. No field marketing presence there. No surprise, after four years and over $10 million invested, that all they'd accomplished was a hodgepodge, "home brew" management decision system with barely a shred of field sales usability. And when someone naively asked, "Will this system work for the field?" the snappy reply was, "As long as they can print their direct mail letters, they'll be happy."

Two fries short of a Happy Meal, that one.

They all need a reality check. So does their organization, which stands to spend millions more for the privilege of falling further behind the competition—and losing a good piece of their sales force when they belatedly introduce this mess that should never see the light of day.

For organizations unaccustomed and unprepared to consider relationship management needs first, CRM and attendant customer-driven marketing strategies will inevitably clash with the corporate culture. Attempts to bend the rules and implement CRM as a corporate system with relationship management tentacles usually follow. Better that such organizations not attempt to implement CRM until they're ready and able to change their internal priorities. And if they do, they'd better bring along giant dustpans and big brooms to clean up all the messes.

> **CRM is not a flexible and forgiving environment when its focus drifts far from relationship-management needs to management-information wants.**

CRM is not a flexible and forgiving environment when its focus drifts far from relationship-management needs to management-information wants, or when it's turned into a big stick for keeping sales in line. Done right, it's an enormously powerful tool. Used as a backdrop for filling corporate information larders or beating up on sales, CRM actually can do lots of damage to the organization. And a good measure of that damage is only reversible over time—the time it takes to win back the trust of your sales and service people, which won't be anytime soon.

Systems

Hey, we got through "Information Flow" without getting more than ankle deep in techie-talk. So let's try to do the same for CRM-related information systems—before we get to CRM software.

To clear up the confusion about CRM-related systems, we do have to risk engaging in a bit more plastic pocket-liner patter. So put your seat belt back on and pay close attention to the road we're taking. I'll try to keep it light. (If you're an IT professional, please skip this section entirely. You won't learn a thing by reading it, and you'll save yourself a severe case of heartburn from reading incomplete, oversimplified descriptions of stuff that's near and dear to your heart. I just want sales, service and marketing folks to have a concept of what you're thinking and talking about in your language while they're thinking and talking in their languages about CRM.)

Here we go. You're a one-person office. You have one computer. That computer has what's called an operating system, or OS. (And now you know how they came up with DOS—it stands for "da operating system.") Your operating system is probably Windows 98®. Or maybe Windows 95®. If it's Mac, you've been drawing pictures instead of reading, so you can nod out again. This operating system provides core commands like "turn on" and "turn off," "print this" and "fetch that file from the hard drive." It also provides the basic user interface— what users see and whether they enter keyboard commands, use a mouse, or both. That's why Windows looks so different from DOS on your screen.

Now, you can't do much with just Windows alone. You need application programs that perform some task or other, probably a whole bunch of related tasks. You buy these programs at Software R Us. Or from a mail-order catalogue. Or from your business computer resource. Unless they came preloaded on your computer. But most of those preloaded programs aren't very businesslike, except for Microsoft Office®, which unfortunately is being supplanted as "free software" with your computer purchase by shovel-loads of Internet garbage.

Nice and cozy. You. Your operating system. Your application programs. An island unto yourself. Until you plug a phone line into the modem that came with your computer and sign up for Internet service. Suddenly, you're a cyber-citizen.

Oh, I almost forgot. When you purchased Microsoft Office for all your office work it came with a personal contact and calendar management program named "Outlook™." Neat program. Exchanges data with your little hand-held computer you carry to meetings. And it has it's own little database, everything it needs, self-contained, and it links right up to your existing word processor. Anyway, you grow. A second person comes to work in your office. Or maybe you had to go out and get an office so a second person could work with you. Now you have two computers. But only one can be hooked up to the printer at any one time. And exchanging files by trading diskettes gets old fast, especially when you create this humongo file with lots of graphics that won't split, but that's too big for a diskette. So you buy two network cards, one for each computer, and a network cable to run between your computers. You spend five minutes installing the cards and a day-and-a-half loading this dumb software program that came with the cards, plus another half-day and three tech support calls configuring Windows 98 for network use. Now you have a peer network. You can both use the same printer. You can rifle through each other's files. Best of all, you get to keep using all of your existing applications software. But you can't send each other e-mail without using telephone lines and the Internet— to travel six feet.

Oh, you and your partner tried to network Outlook. No dice. Takes a more sophisticated network setup. Or you tried to network some other little contact/calendar manager you bought that's supposedly more sophisticated than Outlook. Same deal. So you ran down to Software R Us and bought two copies of a more expensive contact/calendar manager that says it networks. Dump city, in some cases. But let's say you're lucky and bought one that does network, at least some of the time. Dicey, but it will do.

Your business blossoms. You add more employees. Each one gets a computer with a network card and a network cable running to these network hubs you had to buy to plug everybody into one "peer-to-peer" (no server) network. But then things start getting weird. No one knows which file is on what computer. People take to shouting, "Who moved the blankety-blank file for XYZ company off my hard drive?" and the like. So you grab the Yellow Pages, look under "Computer Consultants," and call the one with the least obnoxious ad.

The consultant arrives, strokes his beard, and says, "You need a real network. A LAN (local area network). I can handle this for you." Actually, your peer-to-peer network is really a LAN, but no one calls it that because then what would they call a LAN with a central server? Anyway, a few weeks and many thousands of dollars later, you have a server that holds everyone's files in a common directory. You can get into everyone else's files. But they can't get into yours, thanks to this neat security system. You still get to keep your Windows operating system and application programs. But you now have this less-than-novice-friendly software program that *administers* the network. Pain in the butt.

But on the brighter side, you went back to Software R Us and said, "We want the best contact manager on the shelf." You got it. Bought one for every person dealing with customers, sales and service both. Runs great on the network, too. Uses something called a "shared directory." Everyone uses their own software but shares the same database. Reps on the road can even tie in their laptops to update data. But the service people are griping. They say they can't use it because it's set up wrong for service calls. Can't do much analysis on it, either. "I thought that dumb clerk said this was the best. Friend of mine keeps showing me how they can pinpoint what's going wrong and what's going right in their sales process. Why can't we?"

Growth, growth, growth. Before long, your network has slowed to a crawl. It takes five minutes to download the fax template to order lunch. That contact manager you bought can't hold all the customer data you're generating either. Gotta do something different. This time you call the biggest ad in the Yellow Pages. Slick consultant. Nice clothes. Gives you two choices. Go with a real network, as in "client-server" (upscale LAN with software resident of the server)—or install a new age web-based network that gets you right into e-commerce.[6] But you can also do e-commerce along with the client-server deal, and web-based makes you think of spiders, so you opt for client-server. You gasp at the price. And you gasp even louder when you hear that you'll have to add yet another operating system called "Windows 2000" at the server level. You sense that all this is getting out of hand.

But you do it. New network server (that's a computer) operating on Windows 2000. Then there's this razzle-dazzle new question-writing language that queries your new SQL Server database that holds all your data. "Wait a minute," you complain, "I'm confused as hell."

"Relax," your consultant says, "don't sweat the details." Under your breath you say, "Don't sweat getting paid."

"But," your consultant adds, "that store-bought contact management program wasn't designed to run over your client-server network with your SQL Server database. Besides, it's a

---

[6] Not to get any more technical than absolutely necessary—but an oversimplified definition of "web-based" is putting software and data on a central web server and accessing both using a glorified browser like you use to access the Internet.

dinosaur. Today's software integrates contact and calendar management with sales, customer service and marketing functions. They call this stuff "Customer Relationship Management software," you've heard of it, "CRM." You can't buy it in stores—but a good buddy of mine is a CRM consultant. He can help you." You sense it coming and grab your wallet.

Sure enough, the CRM software programs that the CRM consultant shows you cost more per user than you invested to start the whole damn business (if you ignore the credit card "loans" you took out). And there's this CRM "server" license that's going to cost 15 grand (more than you invested including the credit cards). But hey, you've got the dough now. Then the other shoe drops. Your friendly CRM consultant informs you that you're not ready to pick a CRM system yet because you don't know yet what you need. Something about "customer relationship strategies" and "redefined functional roles" and "redesigned process flow" and "new data maps." Bleary-eyed by now, you just roll over and say, "Find out what we need to do, BUT DO IT FAST."

But then you learn from Ms. Consultant that this CRM stuff isn't just about software. In fact, software is much further down the food chain than lots of other changes you're about to make to get closer to your customers—because that's what CRM is all about, rather than just software. You want to scream, "All I want is some software," when something inside you screams back, "I want software because I want to get closer to my customers, and what fool would try using *software* to lead their business in a more customer-centric direction?" "But we can buy software right now," your impatient side yells back. "But we can just go and change our company 'right now.'" All the yelling starts hurting your inner ears.

But you finally let go of this "software first" stuff. And you swallow hard yet one more time and agree to devote lots o' time over the next three months to planning (hey, that's lots less time than the big guys spend, or should). We'll come back to planning later. But suffice it to say that at the end of all this planning and resulting re-design of functional activities and re-engineering of work processes, you discover that you're about to put lots of information on a server that's accessible to customers, your growing field sales staff, even your vendors—all over the Internet. And you're going to have to link this server and its data to your internal servers and data and yada yada yada.

CRM-speak has to include more than a little IT-speak.

Yeah, that "web-based" stuff you resisted rushing into before—before you knew what you were going to do with it. Hey, you're even going to sell stuff over the Internet—and buy stuff to fulfill new orders. Whoopee!

That's enough of Technology 101.

Dog-ear these pages so you can reread them before your next meeting with IT. Hopefully you'll be better able to understand what they're babbling about (and when they're babbling), and they'll be better able to understand what you're babbling about. For every time you've said, "They just don't understand customers," IT has said, "They just don't understand technology." Enough of that. From both sides.

CRM-speak has to include more than a little IT-speak. Hope you grasped several of the key words. Besides, all you have to do is mix in an occasional word of theirs while you're speaking your language. That works.

Software

Have you been waiting with baited breath for this part? Shame on you. To bastardize a famous quote from the Prez, "It's not the software, stupid." No, I'm not calling you "stupid." I'm just saying that we all have to remind ourselves over and over again to stay on topic when we talk CRM. First and foremost, CRM is a business strategy. However, software is still an important part of the CRM equation, so let's start talking about it.

We've already looked from a distance at the historical development of CRM technology. Now let's press our nose to the glass.

In the early 1980s, "personal information managers" or "PIMs" started showing up. They provided users with calendar management, contact information management, occasionally some assistance in preparing and sending letters and faxes to contacts, and not much more. A program called Sidekick™ was among the first. The original ACT!™ program was probably the best known entry in the PIM market. Until Microsoft Outlook came along in the late 1990s and became lead dog. But that's okay, PIMs had long outlived their usefulness by then in CRM terms (although not for solo acts).

> **To bastardize a famous quote from the Prez, "It's not the software, stupid."**

In the late 1980s, field sales representatives (and their managers) began adopting beefed up PIM programs called "contact managers"— which did everything PIMs did plus tracked sales contact histories for each customer and, significantly for management, sales activities for each sales rep. Collectively, these contact managers and new behaviors they supported became known as "sales force automation" or "SFA." And when sales management or company management tried to force these programs on sales representatives who resented big brother watching over them, they became known as "sales force alienation." GoldMine®, Maximizer® and beefed up versions of the original ACT! were among the best-known SFA software packages.

In the early-to-mid 1990s, the emergence of both new network technologies and methods of synchronizing data on field sales laptops with central databases spawned higher-level SFA systems, often called "enterprise SFA." "Enterprise" was a misnomer, given that these systems couldn't integrate with anything else, but big talk often sells well, and it did here. Before long you couldn't walk across the SFA software playing field without stepping on new software programs from this company and that.

There was so much software for sale that trade shows sprung up to help developers sell it. And then publications ranging from SFA newsletters to a real magazine sprung up. Everything was exploding—except the sales results of SFA users. Which weren't growing much, if at all. Which caused software companies and corporate management to point their fingers at *stubborn* sales people who wouldn't willingly leave the "good ol' boys" days and couldn't see their laptops over their beer bellies. Which caused sales people to point fingers back at makers of *stupid* software systems that did everything except what sales needed and *greedy* managers who wanted sales to work twice as hard so they could work half as hard. What a mess.

But it was a profitable mess for lots of software sellers. So they kept on selling. However, it was thoroughly unprofitable if not outright injurious, to most companies trying to use this stuff. So they gradually woke up and realized something was wrong. Then they did what companies do when something's wrong. They brought in consultants to fix things. Many of whom went into cahoots with software sellers to get a slice of the pie. But some of them knew the score and said it. Out loud. "SFA is a flop."

Truth is, SFA *was* a flop. Most of it was a feeble attempt to build better customer relationships through software. Reminds me of "better living through chemistry." Pure hallucination. Fact is, building better relationships with customers requires a complex combination of new initiatives from all corners of the company. We could automate the daylights out of sales—but that wouldn't do much good without participation by customer service, marketing and back-office functions such as accounting, manufacturing, logistics, etc., etc. That wasn't exactly news to many of us who'd been hanging around relationship marketing waiting for effective technology to finally show up—but it sure surprised the hell out of lots of SFA software folks, who finally started developing a new genre of more integrated software, the CRM stuff.

> **Building better relationships with customers requires a complex combination of new initiatives from all corners of the company.**

It was around 1997 that the software guys started getting serious about expanding what had been SFA to include customer service. Actually, service functions had been automated for years—but almost always as part of back-office accounting or manufacturing information systems, which did little to deliver value to customers. With the advent of CRM, we grabbed hold of customer service's swivel chair and rotated service around to face the customer and make protecting the *customers'* interests as important as protecting the company's interests. 'Course, doesn't take a genius to figure out that putting service and sales on the same software system wouldn't by itself change customer service's charge to protect the company first, the customer second. That would require new, management-led, customer relationship strategies. But we were too impatient for that.

So, with only a half-baked relationship between sales and service established, we next rolled marketing into the equation. Or did marketing roll itself into the equation? But mainstream marketing, database marketing included, barely has a clue about building customer relationships. Which is why adding what traditional marketers started calling "marketing automation" to sales and service automation often pulled CRM further from its purpose—*bettering customer relationships.* Hey, bottom line, buyers are tired of hearing from sellers—whether by advertising, direct mail, telemarketing, e-mail or Internet banner ads and such. They want sellers to hear from them—and to listen. Most of what we called "marketing automation" is still little more than seeing how often we could say how much how easily to buyers with the deepest pockets. That ain't listening. And that ain't CRM. That's more old worms in new cans.

> **Mainstream marketing, database marketing included, barely has a clue about building customer relationships.**

But fear not, despite the frequent failure of CRM technology to connect still disconnected sales, service and marketing functions, the software folks started throwing grappling hooks over the front-office/back-office wall—to see if they could snare some back-office data and dump it into CRM. Plus, they began a mass migration to "e-CRM"—throwing the whole mess up on the Internet (or on internal web databases) so every CRM user could just dial up, get on the network, and access not only their data but most of their software as well. Hey, with just a browser on the laptop, any bloke can connect with centrally located software that performs functions on centrally located data, *n'est pas?* Yah, sure. "Where do you want me to stick that phone jack, buddy?"

Talk about trying to fly before you can crawl. But that's where we are today with CRM software. Very few developers have yet *effectively* melded sales and service automation. Most are busily scabbing on marketing functions that don't much further, and often detract from, the core mission of CRM. And virtually all are frenetically adopting bucket-loads of half-baked functionality to use over the Internet and/or internal web-based networks. Not to mention trying to do with software what can only be accomplished by fully-implemented, multi-faceted business strategies.

Now for the bad news.

Not to paint with too broad a brush—because there *are* some responsible CRM software sellers in the market—but the majority of software vendors are still lying to their customers about their products. Big time. There's so much suspect technology out there that Jack Webb couldn't arrest it all.

One more thing, and I'll let up—I promise. Just because CRM software is *supposed* to help develop positive customer relationships doesn't mean that CRM software developers subscribe to that principle. *Au contraire*. In fact, the majority of CRM software companies practice old-style, foot-in-the-back selling. Sell and run, instead of sell and service. They virtually have to if they're selling software before customer relationship strategies are formulated, because customers don't know yet what they really need. *Caveat emptor,* eh?

We'll talk more later about software selection, but let's first do a claim-reality analysis of common CRM software industry claims.

Claim

Universal applicability: The software industry story line goes, "whatever your business and CRM requirements, our software package will adapt to meet your needs."

Reality

Gotta make this quarter's sales projections: CRM software is not silly putty. It doesn't bend whatever way you want it to. In fact, one best-selling system whose maker claims complete adaptability is among the most restrictive—and thereby least likely to meet your specific requirements.

Claim

Our software performs all functions equally well: We do sales as well as service, service as well as marketing, marketing as well as sales yada yada yada.

Reality

Most CRM software is keyed to a particular function: Virtually every CRM system on the market has its roots in sales automation, customer service, database marketing or occasionally field service. And *full functionality* is often achieved by buying a software company whose product is strong in another area and scabbing the two systems together. That's why I prefer systems developed internally, by one company. But they're the exception.

Claim

CRM software has to be web-based and thin-client[7] to be good: Any CRM system that doesn't utilize a central, web-based database accessed through a browser interface is yesterday's news.

Reality

We're too into web technology to care much about system users: Today's web-based systems, with rare exceptions, suffer from one or most or all of these shortcomings: remote users need to connect to the web to have full-system functionality and connect to the web to access all their data; all users suffer some loss of system speed (over a good, client-server system); substitution of simplicity for functionality. Web browsers are great in some situations—such as working with independent sales reps, distributors and dealers—but a pure web system usually shortchanges field sales and call center operatives. Often severely.

Claim

Our software will help you redesign your work processes: Our software helps you plan your CRM implementation. So it's okay to buy software before you know how you're going to use it.

Reality

We can't wait for you to be ready to buy software: New CRM work processes (and requirements for supporting technology) flow from new CRM strategies that drive new functional activities. Buying software contributes nothing to the CRM planning process—and only encourages taking shortcuts around planning.

---

[7] Meaning individual stations, whether laptops or desktops, only require a browser to run the CRM software.

Again, I want to emphasize that there *are* some responsible software sellers in the market. Remedy and Epicor (Clientele), both of whom I've consulted with, are two. Optima Technologies, which does as much systems integration work as CRM stuff (a handy skill), is a third. And there are more that I can't personally vouch for that have good reputations. What makes these companies different? They do stuff like willingly and responsibly slowing down the sales cycle when they see their potential client is not yet ready to buy software; investing in reseller training so their VARs (value-added reseller) can help clients plan CRM implementations, not letting product out on the street until it's rock solid, intelligently blending web functionality into their systems rather than going off on a web toot because it's trendy, and even telling potential customers they're not the right software for the customer's application. These outfits and others like them may put themselves at a competitive disadvantage in the short run—but with so many systems from so many vendors blowing up out there, they should prosper in the long run.

And there's some more good news on the CRM software front. Some really big news. From the start, CRM software has been built and priced for big customers. The middle market has been badly underserved. And small business? Forget it. But help is on the way—and from a totally unexpected source. Microsoft.

Hey, Microsoft is a long-time client, although not for anything related to CRM software, and I had nothing remotely to do with this. But Microsoft turned Office 2000 into one hell of a development platform—a fact we virtually stumbled upon out of desperation when faced with developing CRM software for a client with a unique set of technology support requirements, stuff that's far afield of any CRM system on the market today.

With Outlook and SQL Server 7 as a base, a skilled Visual Basic programmer can take the new Office 2000 toolkit and do some incredible stuff. You can spend a lot doing this—if your requirements are demanding—but you can also cover the basics for a lot less than you'd shell out to buy an existing package and modify it to meet your needs. And that's a bright ray of light shining out at small business organizations and even some middle market companies as well.

Because I love working with middle market and small business clients, which can handle CRM-induced change more readily than big business, this is

> **The "Outlook solution" may just kick the stuffing out of the competition on the small-system side of the CRM market.**

good news for me. But I'm afraid it's gonna be bad news for CRM software sellers trying to present their products as practical for the middle market and even small business. Because the "Outlook solution" may just kick the stuffing out of the competition on the small-system side of the CRM market—and even in some middle market space.

Opportunity

Hey, with all the hard history behind CRM, its still difficult present and all the technology issues—it must have a *big* future to keep us keeping on, no? Yes, big indeed.

How big is *big?* Damn big. Not golf ball or tennis ball or baseball or softball big. But beach ball big. As long as someone takes the time and trouble to fully inflate it before putting it into play. But think back to the "Introduction" of this book and the high failure rate of CRM projects. Obviously, lots of beach balls are sitting out there deflated. Some just need inflating. Others have holes in them that need patching. Some are beyond patching. But even if you have to start over again from scratch, CRM is worth it.

Why does CRM have such astonishing potential? So much potential that so many organizations continue to try it, despite the risks? I could go on and on about all the wonderful outcomes CRM can produce. Write a whole book about it. But I won't. I won't because there's way too much "CRM dreaming" going on out there, and we need to knock the stars out of our eyes and do more than talk the talk.

That said, some of this stuff is too good not to talk about. So I will. For a while. Then it's back into the challenges and more messy stuff.

CRM has such an amazing upside for many reasons—but consider these six in particular.

1. **Sales and marketing are still waiting for the industrial revolution.** Actually, they're still in the stone age, but they're right at the mouth of the cave. From a process management standpoint, they have nowhere to go but up, and they have a staggering amount of room for improvement. After decades of management neglect, the revenue-producing side of business is getting a heap of attention. In fact, a heap more than many are prepared to handle, because with that attention comes vastly increased accountability and measurability.

   Before long, sales and marketing will be evaluating and re-evaluating their processes just like manufacturing and financial people do today. The goal? To develop the discipline required to develop and maintain long-term customer relationships, instead of flying around from ad to ad and sale to sale. And that's a job tailor-made for CRM's process management potential.

2. **CRM can be your competitive edge.** While more and more organizations are attempting to jump on the CRM bandwagon, most of them land on their you-know-what. And if you figure that most companies, especially in the middle and small business markets, still haven't taken their first leap, that leaves the small minority that have successfully implemented CRM in a distinctly superior competitive position.

Hey, anytime you have a wide disparity among competing organizations in adoption of a critical new methodology, you're going to see winners and losers. The wider the disparity, the wider the gap between winners and losers. Just ask American car makers who failed to adopt modern process management techniques in the 1980s about that.

3. **CRM benefits both sides of the ledger.** And the benefits on either the income or expense side are sufficient to quickly pay off investment in a well-designed, well-deployed CRM system. Add up increased sales from current customers, better customer retention and customer acquisition focused on high lifetime value customer—add to that decreased selling costs, reduced marketing and marketing communication expenditures, reduced intra-company communication expense, plus lots more—and the payoff can be big. Really big.

4. **CRM improves throughput across the organization.** Hey, it's not just sales, service and marketing that work more effectively and efficiently in a CRM environment—virtually everyone in every functional area does. Why? Because over time we've managed to design virtually every business activity to meet internal needs. Not customer needs. And you know what? Not centering work activities around customers creates huge inefficiencies that drive up operating costs. Don't believe me? Then sit down with a pencil and reroute the flow of information in your company to better serve customers, rather than individual departments. What happens? If you enact these changes, you'll take a sizeable chunk out of your annual investment in

IT—because corporate information systems are wastefully designed around meeting departmental needs, rather than servicing customers.

5. **CRM can be the synapse between traditional sales, service and marketing and the new Internet opportunities.** When our customers are dealing with live people, we can at least pretend that customer information is being captured and properly managed. But when customers begin communicating and transacting with us through multiple channels—in person, telephone, e-mail, Internet, ESP—somehow we gotta meld all this stuff together into one coherent mass (not mess). Then we have to do something intelligent with it. And when customers want information we've kept locked up for so long we can't find the key, we gotta find ways to let them in. And we have to find out where else they want to go and build paths to get there. *Ergo,* customer relationship management and customer information management are becoming the order of the day. Hey, if CRM marketing-types remember to listen, not talk—and if CRM technology-types get focused on blending old channels with new, rather than abandoning old channels for new—CRM is going to play a pivotal role, wherever this crazy ride we're on takes us.

But most important of all.

6. **Customers are demanding CRM.** No, customers aren't grabbing your salespeople by the lapels or calling you or e-mailing you or sending messages via your website demanding CRM by name. But they are demanding what CRM helps you

provide: knowledge of them that's shared by all in the company no matter how it's received, input from them that's "on the record" (their customer record) to help you do business their way, attention to them when *they* want it—and how *they* want it, and access by them to everything they need to know about their orders and projects with you. And they're not kidding about this stuff, either.

Bottom line, customers have had it with self-centered businesses. More than ever before, they've got choices, and they're not hesitating to choose with their feet. So if you want their business, you'd better be prepared to do it their way. And that doesn't mean fawning all over them. It means paying attention to them, knowing them, acting on what you know, and making them part of your business processes—which is damn near impossible to pull off in most businesses without practicing CRM.

In other words, CRM is an opportunity to keep your customers and win as much of their business as possible. Not an opportunity you want to pass up.

Now, I'd really like to end this chapter right here. The customer demands CRM. It's part of the price of being in business today—and especially tomorrow. Enough said. But I'm old enough and hard-bitten enough to know that won't fly. Realistically, most companies are going to evaluate CRM's potential according to what it can do right here and right now—not what CRM will deliver long-term by forging stronger customer relationships. So we'd better evaluate CRM opportunities in those terms. So let's do it, function by function—sales, service, marketing, e-commerce, IT and management.

Sales Opportunities

Process management and process improvement—that's what CRM contributes directly to sales efforts to acquire, develop and retain customers. Okay, some of you will object to this characterization of sales, in particular, as a process. "Hey, selling is a gift. Right?" As we say in Minnesota, "you betcha."

I still remember sitting in a client meeting listening to a VAR for a supposed CRM software system insist that, "Sales is not a process; it's individual to everyone and you can't reduce it to process steps." The client winked at me as we left the room. Unbelievable. But that's how ingrained the view of "sales as a personality aberration" really is. Even some in the very business of supporting the sales process claim they're doing otherwise. What, I don't know.

A sales training manager at one of this country's more successful manufacturers of recreation equipment provided what I consider the last word about the role process plays in sales success. My principal client contact and I were presenting the rough concept of a new CRM system to this training manager and others. We needed this guy's buy-in for successful implementation in field sales—and we were concerned about him, because this individual, who should have been involved from day one, had just been hired.

> **"Salespeople sell by process or by accident. Accidents don't happen often enough."**

So we carefully explained why the proposed CRM system focused so hard on managing sales activities. Fact was, sales process improvement was among the principal opportunities CRM offered this client.

When we finished, he leaned back, thought for a second, turned to my contact and said, "Salespeople sell by process or by accident. Accidents don't happen often enough."

Amen.

To build on that, this same company hired a new sales rep from another industry shortly after. Right off the bat this fellow started making lots of people nervous. For three months (which happened to be the first three month of their fiscal year), this rep barely made a sales call, at least not to sell anything. And he barely sold anything. What was he doing? Building an information base on his customers, their needs, what they would be buying when. And then, methodically, he went to work. At the end of the fiscal year he was onstage receiving a prestigious sales award for being among the top five performers in the company. Unheard of for a first-year rep. Hey, sales effectiveness in their business only came after a long ramp-up period. Supposedly. But effective sales process proved this wrong. Dead wrong.

Although your very best salespeople may appear to have a gift for selling, underneath their gift you'll find a bedrock foundation of steps they take to complete the sale—and maintain the customer relationship over time. They may operate so smoothly and effortlessly that you never see them following these steps. But they are. And they can pull it off without benefit of CRM software or much other technology.

But these are your very best. What about the great middle—your average performers? Lacking that rare marriage of personality and process, which part of the equation would you want them to have? If you've ever been a sales manager, you answered "process" without a moment's hesitation. Why? Because a significant part of the selling process occurs out of sight of the customer—time spent reviewing what customers want us to know about them, scheduling consistent customer contacts when customers want them, pulling together information of specific value to specific customers. All stuff that requires great discipline, the discipline of process, discipline that sales *personalities* rarely have. Do this stuff well and you'll succeed in sales, perhaps even become a sales star, even if you're not a great schmoozer. And I can say that from experience. Because I succeeded in sales despite being a certifiable, Meyers-Briggs introvert. Because I did all the preparation, the research, the customizing and especially the listening and recording required to become a *star*—without a *gift* for selling.

Too global for you? Okay, let's drill down a little more. On a very tangible level, here's what CRM delivers to sales-oriented companies.[8]

Qualification of initial sales inquiries. Picking the wheat from the chaff becomes much easier when each inquiry received turns into a CRM database record, rather than a paper form or worse. Especially considering the high percentage of sales inquiries that come from "tire-kickers." These electronic records help telephone qualifiers increase their speed and accuracy determining who's worth pursuing and who's not. So do branching, onscreen scripts built into their CRM software. And entering into their CRM database high points of their dialog with potential customers preserves information extremely valuable to sales. Then, when leads are qualified and sales-ready, a mouse click or two on the CRM system can assign and transport them to the right sales representatives. Pretty slick. And the telephone folks can even reactivate temporarily non-qualified responses for re-qualification down the road. Really helps maximize the ROI on generating sales inquiries.

Sales call selectivity. Ever wonder why sales people frequently call on relatively low volume accounts rather than key accounts? Happens all the time and for lots of reasons. But this tendency tends to reverse when sales reps rely on database

---

[8] I've listed CRM benefits that accrue to companies with strong field sales presence. But much of this applies to any business that sells person-to-person.

information to work up their call list. Now, that's not to say that sales numbers should be the sole criteria for selecting whom to call on when. When customers *want* reps to call factors in big. And new product introductions and special price offers often require call schedules skewed toward specific product usage and particular customer needs. Taking two minutes to build a CRM database query to find the right customers or prospects to call on at the right time is a heck of a lot more accurate and efficient than leaning back and saying, "Now, let's see"—or, "What sounds good for lunch today?"

Call frequency. How often reps call on customers should flow from customer potential and preference. But, call frequency too often reflects: a rep's like or dislike of specific customer contacts, the customer's *tolerance* of limited attention from the relationship manager, convenience factors, you name it. If you analyze sales calls at year-end to compare call frequency with call impact, you'll usually discover very frequent occurrences of both over coverage and under coverage. CRM can fix that in a wink. A good CRM database will let us calculate optimal call frequency based on projected impact of calls, tempered by customer preference—then adjust frequency with a few mouse clicks or keystrokes when situations change. Big improvement on the "perverse Pareto Principle" that's commonly at work in sales. You know, spending 80% of sales time on 20% of business.

Call focus. Focus is to sales what location is to real estate. How many times have all of us who've "carried the bag" wasted hard-to-schedule sales calls focusing on the wrong products or the wrong needs or the wrong concerns? Too many times to remember. Funny how our mistake dawns on us minutes after the call, when we're finally able to put two and two together. Not that CRM is going to add two and two and give relationship managers the score at the door, but a good database will prompt relationship managers to recall key issues and help establish the right call strategy. Two minutes reviewing a computerized customer record before the call can cut two years off the close—or tell you you'll need a miracle to get a close.

Continuity. No customer likes to hear stuff from their sales rep like, "Did we talk about...?" "Did I mention...?" "Did you ask me...?" or "Now I remember..." Continuity is about being buttoned-down, professional, respectful, competent. It's also about keeping the sales dialog on track from call to call, not wasting half the time remembering where the last call left off or what got discussed. The continuity provided by CRM call histories is particularly helpful in making the transition from one relationship manager to another—without losing sales momentum and accumulated customer knowledge.

More customer time. By definition, more customer time implies less *office* time doing expense reports, call reports, status reports, revised forecasts and whatever else management dreams up. More customer time also involves spending less time doing offline customer work—preparing customer quotes and proposals, product research, customer correspondence, responding to customer inquiries and all that. How do reps shuck all this stuff? Actually, you don't want them to shuck it, at least not most of it. You want to help them do it faster. Much faster. And CRM automation helps sales do office and offline work at warp speed. That'll save a sales rep hours per week, perhaps a day per week.

Improved close ratios. Companies don't up their sales close ratios by training reps in "19 surefire closing techniques" or passing out copies of "I Made a Million Dropping My Pen on Ready-to-Sign Contracts." Increased close ratios result from understanding which opportunities are most likely to close and for what reasons—and pursuing them accordingly. Practicing CRM greatly enhances that understanding.

Can CRM predict successful closes? Not infallibly. But sales reps who take the time to populate customer and prospect data records can read situations much more clearly than those who don't—allowing them to focus on their best opportunities and walk away from long shots. A simple CRM spread sheet program tied to each customer's record can calculate future value based on the probability of getting the business, at what price and for what volume. Running that report will not only reshape call schedules, but also automate sales forecasting and increase forecasting accuracy. And when you factor in relative profitability values—wow!

Increased lifetime value. The sales world is full of "one-order wonders"—sales reps who excel at persuading customers to place a first order, then lose interest in these customers. Reps who operate this way thrive on "the thrill of the hunt." Going back just isn't as much fun (especially if they only get commission on new customers for the first year or even less). Plus, "one-order wonders" aren't particularly careful about the claims they make to secure that first shot, and they don't want to return to face the music. Bottom line, these reps produce negative bottom line, because customer acquisition costs almost always exceed first order profits. Truth is, in many business lines, offsetting customer acquisition costs requires a year or two worth of orders.

CRM is the perfect antidote to "sell and run" sales tactics. CRM philosophy emphasizes sales activities *after* the first sale. CRM work processes, supported by CRM technology, provide the discipline required to stretch the sales cycle over customer lifetime. And if all else fails, CRM activity measurements tell management who's managing customer relationships effectively and who's not.

Lower sales force turnover. Hey, we know how expensive replacing customers can be. Same applies to replacing sales reps—particularly after you've invested bundles training them in on complex products. And rep churn has a big hidden expense behind it—customer churn.

Good salespeople are hard to find, harder to hire and even harder to keep. What can we do about that? We can't increase the birthrate of star sales talent. We can't clone sales stars. And even if we could, genetic re-engineering is even slower than corporate re-engineering. So we have to do the next best thing—decrease dependence on highly visible (and highly marketable) star performers by increasing productivity among the middle echelon of moderately talented, less-than-superstar relationship managers.

CRM does that in spades by,

- Tracking and measuring individual sales process steps to identify best practices that midlevel reps should emulate.

- Identifying process problems for individual reps, giving management the opportunity to provide highly targeted training support to address weaknesses.

- Predicting the future success of new hires, allowing management to end a terminal situation long before their intuition is confirmed by poor sales outcomes.

- Keeping reps focused (in part by keeping their managers focused). A rep who can't get or stay focused is not long for his or her position.

- Providing a challenge to reps that can help keep their jobs fresh and help them maintain a sense of personal growth.

- Giving them sales tools superior to what they'll get in their next job.

And I could keep going and make this a long list without breaking a sweat.

One face to the customer. CRM helps multi-line or multidivisional users maintain *one face* to the customer. Sort of like the left hand knowing what the right hand is doing. Which prevents one purchasing agent from getting successive calls from six representatives of the same company.

That's enough. You get the picture by now (either that, or you may prefer reading such classics as "Order Them to Sell," "Heel Sales, Heel" or my personal favorite, "101 Top Tricks of Top Sales Performers."

Service Opportunities

In most organizations, customer service is much further along the work process and supporting technology adoption curve than either sales or marketing. But does that mean CRM opportunities in service are incidental or peripheral? *Au contraire.*

CRM does have less to offer customer service per se than it offers the other two disciplines. At least right now it does. It's even true in some industries (the airline industry for example) that customer service has relatively little linkage with sales or marketing. But the absence of customer service involvement would leave a gaping hole in the whole concept of CRM. In fact, it's doubtful that CRM could stay afloat most places without intense service involvement.

> **How do you present one face to the customer when the two most frequent contact points for customers can't communicate?**

After all, how do you effectively marry all of your customer information if you leave out some of the most important interactions with customers? How can you build strong customer relationships if face-contact folks don't know when their customers are having problems? And how do you present *one face* to the customer when the two most frequent contact points for customers can't communicate? Pretty hard. And multiply that difficulty a gazillion times when more customer service and customer interaction switches to the Internet. Then you've got to blend *machine contact* with human contact and make sure each knows what's happened on the other channel.

Near term, the major customer service opportunities in CRM involve sharing information between sales and service on a real-time or near real-time basis. Theoretically, we can accomplish this by building data links between traditional customer service information systems, which are typically tied to accounting or manufacturing, and CRM systems. But practically, their respective technology environments are so dissimilar that the difficulty forging these links deters organizations from even trying. Besides, most customer service departments, even today, report through accounting or manufacturing or operations or somewhere else in the back office. Shifting customer service's information management support to CRM is tantamount, to many back-office folks, to shifting their reporting responsibility out to the front office—through sales and marketing. For many back offices, that's hard to swallow, no matter how much good it might do the company. And I'll let you in on a little secret. These back-office fears are well founded—because that's exactly what will happen (or should) happen once service shifts over to CRM in formation management.

So, anyone suggesting that service adopt CRM technology instead of remaining tied to the back office may be subject to catching some flack—and hearing lots of "can'ts" and "won'ts." But before yielding to the "more pain than gain" view of tying sales and service together, consider the opportunities.

- Informing sales immediately about service issues so they can intervene in the situation and possibly prevent a customer loss.

- Building customer loyalty through service issues rather than having it erode because a customer has a beef.

- The relative costs of keeping customers versus replacing them. Marketing pundits now project the "cost of keeping" at 10% or not much more of the cost to replace.

- The sense of *one company* projected by integrating sales and service data, which sends a powerful message to customers that "you've got your act together."

And think further, on the expense side of the ledger, about:

- Service understanding what commitments sales has made—for example in areas such as information systems or process control equipment, where sales may advise clients to expect problems if they don't change already-installed system elements.

- Service knowing who's in charge on the customer side, in order to respond proactively (or ask sales to do so) when an individual customer contact employs relationship-breaking tactics or blames the seller for user problems.

But most importantly, linking service to sales means:

- Service understands the relative importance of the customers they're dealing with.

A mishap at one of our top ten mega-banks is a wonderful, or awful, example of the importance of service knowing customer status. A customer of this financial institution—which was already considering the installation of a CRM information system shared by sales and service—walked into a branch bank and asked to co-sign a new car loan for his college-student daughter. He picked up an application, completed it with his daughter, then returned it. The paperwork went to the service area that evaluates loan applications, and the service person rejected the application.

End of story? Hardly. The gentleman who walked in to inquire about the loan didn't say, "Aw shucks," when he got the rejection. He yanked all $15 million of his trust funds out of this particular financial institution. Instead of presenting *one face* to the customer, this bank was two-faced. And when the customer didn't like one of those faces, he cut off both. *Sayonara.*

This financial institution learned from the experience. Following this incident, work on CRM proceeded post haste. Unfortunately, many organizations would blame a customer loss like this on *fate,* rather than lousy customer information management.

One more aspect of melding sales and service functions together in CRM merits your attention. In organizations with a direct (company-employed) field sales force, customer service agents often *adopt* the salespeople they work with and do everything possible to

Service reps have a rough time leaving for a new post with inferior communication and customer information management facilities.

help them out, particularly by sharing information they've received over the phone with *their* reps. It's a wonderful thing to see. Maintaining two unlinked customer databases—one for sales and one for service—makes this type of cooperative communication difficult to maintain. Heck, impossible.

Integrating sales and service functions, and especially their data, empowers customer service representatives to accomplish much more than patiently taking a pounding at the hands (or mouths) of irritated customers. And it helps keep service personnel on the job. Service reps, just like their sales counterparts, have a rough time leaving for a new post with inferior communication and customer information management facilities. Think about that.

As for long-term CRM opportunities in customer service, let's put it this way. Dive into the Internet without a customer relationship plan with a strong customer service component, and your customers will make you pay. Just say, "We'll put the information on their website and leave you with 'self-service' only," and they'll make you burn—as many *e-tailers,* who have beat hasty retreats back into *live* customer service, have already discovered. But virtually every company that provides customer service is going to wind up with multiple channels—live over the phone, over the Internet, via e-mail—hey, even face to face.

CRM planning is what's going to guide you in melding these channels. CRM technology is the tool to bring all the data together so the left channel knows what the right is doing. And without it, you're dead. How's that for a benefit.

Marketing Opportunities

Don Peppers and Martha Rogers already wrote the book on CRM marketing opportunities—*The One To One Future, Building Customer Relationships One at a Time*.[9] They followed it up with a couple more— *Enterprise One to One*[10] and *The One to One Field Book*.[11]

Primed us, maybe, but that dang pump still ain't working as often or as well as it should. And for a good reason. We've been missing both the methodology and tools needed to get closer and stay closer to customers. Now we have them—with CRM technology. Reality is starting to catch up with theory, practicality with possibility.

But here's the rub. As you scroll down the list of CRM-based marketing opportunities below, you'll wince just thinking about how unwelcome many of these opportunities will be to marketers. Not to all marketers, but unwelcome to media mavens unable to discriminate between marketing and media advertising; unwelcome to creative types who can't imagine how a salesperson could casually compose an e-mail message to a select customer that would yield more sales than their award-winning ad or direct mail piece; unwelcome to direct marketers who still can't imagine that something else is the future of marketing. Hey, some of these database dunderheads are still trying to frame the Internet as a database marketing media. Go figure.

So catch your breath or shield your eyes—as the case may be—here it comes.

Less media advertising. Placing less reliance on media advertising is a very big marketing opportunity. Think about media advertising's inefficiencies. Its impersonal manner. Its dependency on "one message suits all" creative. Its ambient

---

[9] Ibid.

[10] *Enterprise One To One*, Doubleday, 1997

[11] With Bob Dorf, Doubleday, 1998.

noise level that drives customers crazy. Know what? Advertising is an excellent example of how less could be more. Less money spent on advertising, more money to spend on more productive marketing methods. Less emphasis on advertising, more attention paid to information-driven interaction with customers. Heck, marketing could regain a good measure of the respectability it's lost just by listening to customers, rather than advertising at them. Advertising—it's like a marketing head with the ears chopped off.

CRM, in contrast, is about ears. It's all ears, big memory and the capability to process and act on what it hears. Because CRM listens so well, we can whisper the right messages back to customers—rather than screaming a generic message to the world. And that translates as less direct mail, as well.

> **Because CRM listens so well, we can whisper the right messages back to customers.**

Yeah, I've dumped more than a few pieces of junk mail in most of your mailboxes. But I've reformed. Direct marketers keep saying, "There's no junk mail, just misdirected mail, and we're constantly learning more about our customers and what they want to receive." Ya, sure. And when I open our mailbox I slap my knee and say, "You betcha."

Direct marketers sneak around to get information—from credit files, credit card records, census data, tax files, telephone books, driver licenses, fishing licenses, magazine subscriptions, trade show registrations, birth certificates, garbage cans…and now from sites you visit on the Internet. But they're afraid to ask you for it. They're unwilling to let you decide what you want them to know. If they did, they couldn't mail five gazillion pieces of direct mail a year, call you during dinner 17 times a week, fax you stuff you could care less about, and now jam up your e-mail box. And then some presses would grind to a halt.

So would some mega-computers. Some phone banks would fall silent. Some trees would be left standing. Dinners would be eaten hot. E-mail would be our own again. And long-suffering targets of direct marketing would dance in the streets.

Less spending. Dare we say it? Look at how much automakers spend on advertising for new customers—and how little they spend to keep the ones they have. Hey, it costs the car biz $500 just to bring two feet into the dealership. Car dealers adopting a CRM mentality would change the dynamics of the entire business. Just think about feeling like you're walking on

> **Car dealers adopting a CRM mentality would change the dynamics of the entire business.**

asphalt, not grease, when you walk onto a car lot. What a change in customer mindset. Think about car dealers using information systems (rather than match book covers and paper napkins) to track current customers according to their tastes, their preferences, how long they typically keep a car or when their lease ends. What a repeat sales opportunity, without having to spend big media bucks to bring you back again. Add in tracking customers who came close but bought another make. What fertile and economical marketing ground, especially if customer experience with that other make is less than fully satisfactory.

And I'd be remiss not to mention that turnover costs caused by the extraordinary high migration rate of car salespeople would come down if car reps lost their customer databases every time they moved, thanks to use of CRM databases.

Less customer churn. Having a stable, happy customer base drastically reduces customer acquisition costs. And that helps marketing every bit as much as it helps sales. Happy customers who share good experiences with other customers are very powerful marketing tools, perhaps *the* most powerful.

Definitely more powerful than actors or phony doctors saying good things on TV.

More business from current customers. Effective customer development eases the pressure and expense of constant new-customer acquisition. That allows marketers to step back, think and work strategically, rather than being in a constant flurry of activity trying to bolster this quarter's numbers.

Less obsession with *brand*. Here we go. More blasphemy. At least to some die-hard believers in mass marketing. But letting CRM help us get off the brand kick is a huge opportunity. Look at it this way. Brand strength may be the next best thing to having knowledge-based relationships with customers. But it's a distant second to the power of positive relationships.

Brand barely appears on the "impact-on-customers" radar screen—except in marketing environments like household commodities where maintaining individual customer relationships is economically impractical. For packaged-goods marketers, fine. They need to rely on brand strength. But for automobile marketers, appliance marketers, computer manufacturers, capital-goods manufacturers, most consumer- and business-service marketers—brand strength can't compete with customer information-driven relationship building for impact on customers. And all this talk about "building customer relationships with brands?" People are passionate about other people and ideas and even art, but not about advertising images. "Brand relationships" are the marketing equivalent of hugging telephone poles. Let's leave relationships for human interaction.

Hey, add this all up and you have a CRM bonanza in marketing just waiting for you. All you have to do is run the gauntlet to get there. No sweat.

E-Commerce Opportunities

Speaking of human interaction, as we just were, let's talk about machine interaction—traffic across the Internet, your extranet, wherever. And let's talk sense about it. Hey, doing business how customers want to do business helps build and cement relationships—to a point. But, and this is a big but, once everyone's doing e-commerce, then it's expected. It's your ticket of admission. But relationships are about what makes you *different* to customers, what makes you special. Me too stuff doesn't qualify. And that's why I'm not making a big deal about e-commerce and CRM. The window of competitive opportunity with e-commerce is short—Randy Neumann short. And if you base your CRM strategy primarily on e-commerce, you're going to be e-specially sorry.

> **If you base your CRM strategy primarily on e-commerce, you're going to be e-specially sorry.**

Having said that, CRM does let you build a comprehensive customer interaction log across all channels. But tread lightly here, as well. A growing majority of customers consider tracking their Internet contacts below the "you were there," "you asked about" or "you bought" level an invasion of their privacy. Hey, pulling all this data together to the nth degree of detail may look like a marketer's panacea—but step over the line and you're toast.

A more productive method of integrating e-commerce into CRM in a differentiating, relationship-building manner is through interactive exchanges with customers. Taking care of folks wanting additional product/service information, particularly technical stuff, without wading through a dozen personal contacts to reach a "specialist"—or just someone who knows the score. The quality of this exchange *can* create distinguishing value for customers. And that's a CRM opportunity today, because pretty much everybody trying this today is either dispensing bad or insufficient information, too slow on the draw or both.

Of course, you can use CRM-like technology to manage all manner of e-commerce activity—everything from e-transactions to e-visits. Some CRM technology vendors even claim ownership of all e-commerce. These guys are working hard to restore *hubris* to living language. Hey folks, bottom line—e-commerce is only synonymous with CRM if we take the "R" out. But then it's not "CRM," is it? But then again, a whole lotta CRM technology vendors could give a hoot. To them it's either $$$.com or e.$$$. Which says lots about why they barely understand CRM—if at all.

IT Opportunities

Stop laughing. I mean it. Seriously, CRM *is* a huge opportunity for IT. An opportunity disguised as a problem for some IT folks. But an opportunity nonetheless.

Here's what I mean. Among the most powerful professional experiences I've had, and I've had it a number of times now, is redesigning a client company's information flow around customers—not around the perceived needs of individual functional departments. Better than half the time, implementing this redesign would dramatically shrink the size of the enterprise information system. Impossible? Hardly. Information flow mirrors work process—and work processes designed a department at a time are infinitely more complex than work processes designed to best service the customer, regardless of who winds up doing what.

Streamlining work processes into a continuous flow around customers winds up streamlining information flow the same way.

Streamlining work processes into a continuous flow around customers winds up streamlining information flow the same way. Add in letting CRM systems keep customer information where it's most used and needed—at or near the point of customer contact—and adopting customer-centric CRM across the enterprise *can* skinny down information systems a load.

Notice how I keep hedging, though, with words like "can?" That's because most in IT don't believe any of this yet. It's going to take a few more years (in some cases maybe a few more decades) before most IT departments are willing to talk about designing information flow around customers. That's a shame—and a huge cost to business.

Management Opportunities

Aside from improving the well-being of the company, does CRM offer opportunities to management, which often thinks of itself as operating on a higher level than CRM? *Certainment.*

With very few exceptions, senior management operates either at arm's length from customers, or in total isolation from customers. So when senior executives announce a corporate commitment to "customer intimacy" or "customer focus" or some such, what are the chances they know what they're talking about? Slim to none.

Among the most disappointing CRM experiences I've ever had was with a Fortune 500 manufacturing company of considerable repute. The CEO preached customer intimacy. He even *nurtured* development of CRM, verbally at least. Initiated work on CRM. But the CRM project he initiated had to maintain low altitude in order to avoid hostile fire from corporate fiefdoms that felt empowered to reject any efforts to mess with their *modus operandi* or even their data. These corporate silos turned a deaf ear to any and all suggestions that they subordinate their divisional or departmental interests to benefit the enterprise through CRM.

Many senior executives don't understand that you get buy-in for *how* you're going to get closer to customers, not *whether* you're going to do so.

If you're quicker than I am, which many are, you've realized already that this *nurturing* CEO was the very reason this program had to fly low. He didn't lead. He wouldn't lead. And CRM doesn't happen without the proactive and ever-present backing and protection of senior management. Doing it requires changing internal boundaries, changing workflow, changing information flow and even changing core values of the company, in many cases—stuff that only occurs with a CEO or an executive close to that level leading the charge.

Is that a violation of good management policies, to get out front like that? Some of us call it *leadership*. Unfortunately, many senior executives don't understand that you get buy-in for *how* you're going to get closer to customers, not *whether* you're going to do so. CRM provides senior management with opportunities to lead. Unfortunately, many senior executives aren't up to the task.

Anyway, no sooner did this project appear on screen than heavy flak burst out. It stayed airborne for a while. Then it took a couple of direct political hits and crashed like a plane straight out of a World War II movie.

To use another war analogy, this CRM effort went just like "The Charge of the Light Brigade." We foolishly charged ahead. We all got shot. We got left for dead. Only difference was that nobody wrote any poetry afterwards.

But, you get up and dust yourself off, knowing that you're going to win some and lose some. Better to be in my position than being one of the prime movers internally. Some of them stayed face down.

What a waste. Had this CEO been in better touch with customers, had his senior managers been in better touch with customers, had they appreciated field sales needs, had they..., had they..., had they..., they would have been smart enough and sensitive enough to understand how much value CRM could deliver to their customers. Instead, they're letting their primary competitors beat them to the punch. Big time.

And does CRM put CEOs and senior management in better touch with customers? In two big ways—both directly and indirectly.

Directly, by putting CRM technology and data station on every senior manager's work station. Not for spying or snooping, but so they can read some call reports, feel the pulse of the market, hear what customers are saying verbatim, view the issues management section of the program and learn customer concerns, directly. Altogether, that's powerful learning—and an opportunity to understand what customer intimacy *should* mean—as opposed to shoving our hand deeper into the customer's pocket.

But even more so, CRM can bring management closer to customers indirectly, through osmosis. Getting field managers in better touch with customers and with sales has a domino effect. The more the management layer below *gets it,* the more the layer above does too, and so on up the ladder. CRM has a powerful potential to shorten the distance from customers to senior management. And that's powerful stuff, especially when you consider how many business strategies we base on quantitative "management decision system" data that's totally devoid of input from the most important and powerful force in any business—customers.

CRM can bring management closer to customers indirectly, through osmosis.

Oh, and let's not forget. Improving the overall well-being of the company doesn't do senior management any harm, either.

Whoops, almost forgot one *not-to-forget* CRM management opportunity. CRM gives senior management an opportunity to finally show respect for sales. Only the most narcissistic of senior execs can look at what CRM requires of sales without understanding that the organization needs to put sales and everyone else directly involved in building customer relationships on a high pedestal. CRM asks a lot of our customer contact staff—so much that any reasonable person would bury any past bygones (bad sales jokes included), lend their support and render their respect. But we don't live in a reasonable world—and many executives can't see past their prejudice against those "low-brow folks" in sales that do their dirty work, and some senior managers can't believe anything good would happen were it not for their divine direction.

Guess I'll stop here.

II.
Misunderstanding CRM

Misunderstanding #1: CRM = Software

I'm tempted to say, "Lets not beat a dead horse," and go straight to the next chapter. Unfortunately, this notion that CRM is software isn't a dead horse. It's a dead cat with nine lives. Or a dead something else with 90. It just won't quit. It won't quit, for openers, because there's too much money to be made by *some* CRM software companies selling stuff to unsuspecting customers who don't yet know the cart from the horse (not the dead one).

But there's more than greed supporting the "CRM = software" myth, so let's take at least a quick look at why we have so much trouble seeing CRM for what it is—much more than software.

- **Business prefers dealing in tangibles.** At least American business does. So often it's action over vision, tactics over strategy, do it rather than plan it, next quarter over next year. So it's not surprising that CRM—which requires vision, strategy, planning and perseverance—gets reduced to a software program that will generate ROI this fiscal year. Not surprising, but very disappointing—especially for companies adopting CRM the wrong way for the wrong reasons.

- **Very few CRM software sellers understand CRM.** And even fewer practice it. With very few exceptions, CRM software companies are product-driven, not customer-driven. Product sellers, not solution providers. Just look at their sales techniques. Based on building long-term customer relationships? Not often. Mostly good ol' foot-in-the-back stuff, the very sales style their software should help abolish.

- **Relatively few CRM software systems belong in the marketplace.** If CRM adopters did their planning first, then redesigned their processes, then let their new processes define their software needs—there'd be but a small number of software vendors left, because only a small minority of CRM software systems have much *raison d'être. Informed* customers wouldn't buy much of what's out there.

- **No CRM software works in every situation.** There's no stronger proof that CRM isn't software than the fact that technology requirements for supporting CRM activities vary so widely from company to company. In fact, the whole concept of "universal application" (software that works anywhere) is nothing more than a hollow sales promise. Ironically, we have far too many CRM software systems to choose from, but far too little choice. The real problem is that CRM software companies haven't yet figured out what different types of customers need—especially requirements of customers integrating traditional back-office functions such as order-entry or make-to-order product development or production scheduling or logistics into CRM.

That's enough. That should keep this "dead horse" dead—at least for a chapter or two.

Misunderstanding #2: CRM = e.com

Before getting carried away by the incredible webness of web—and inappropriately attempting to bind CRM to e-commerce, the Internet, extranets, web-based software, etc.—let's look at some cold, hard facts.

- **As long as people are doing the buying, people will be involved in selling.** These predictions of live sales people going the way of the dinosaurs are inane. Of course we're replacing some live sales functions with e-commerce. But customer backlash has already begun in some sectors as we reach customer thresholds for conducting business with computers. E-commerce is still going to grow like crazy, but there are definite limits to its utility in today's and tomorrow's marketplace. Field sales won't be disappearing anytime soon.

- **Customer "self-help" is often a sham—and customers know it.** Customers are already beating up e-tailers, software companies and others over their "convenient," "customer-friendly," "self-service" customer non-service service websites. Bottom line, most of these endeavors are naked attempts to cut service costs. Self-serving rather than self-service. Online customer service *can* benefit customers—UPS and Federal Express are shining examples—but notice that neither of these companies nor other service-sensitive organizations such as Hewlett-Packard and Microsoft *force* customers to use e-service. Another hitch with e-service—taking away a valuable listening post to hear customer complaints takes away the opportunity to hear early warnings about problems that need addressing.

Customer service over the Internet is here to stay, and companies are going to find more and more effective applications. But live customer service is also here to stay.

- **Folks who think the Internet is the end of communication technology development need their heads examined.** The Internet is a highly flawed, *ad hoc,* chewing gum and bailing wire, accidental construct that's fulfilling a need until we come up with a better solution, which probably won't take long. It had better not take long, because the whole thing's going to collapse of its own weight before long. Hey, the Internet is fine for entertainment and shopping and browsing. But my clients deserve better than what it offers. Lots better.

- **Web-based systems architecture is an interim solution.** Those who think web-architecture is the end of systems architecture development—they need their heads examined, too. But I want to take a breather and let someone else set them straight.

> The original trend away from centralized control towards personal computing was, in fact, the correct trend. People should have their own PCs, just as they should have their own toolboxes or their own cars...And web-centric computing is just a data processing version of public mass transit.[12]

Truth be told, web systems architecture is a workaround to help us share data and applications while we develop better solutions. Nope, building giant data dumps (data warehouses) and pouring in vats of data so every user can schlep to the same site to access the stuff real time ain't gonna cut it for long.

That last point reminds me of a meeting I was in with one of our preeminent designers of data warehouses, John Merrill, where he slammed his fist into a conference table over and over again saying, "Do *not* use data warehouses for real time applications." Actually, he wasn't *saying* it, he was yelling it at a group of IT managers bound and determined to keep all customer data in a data warehouse and nowhere else.

- **We can't always be "connected"—and when the time comes that we can, we won't be as Internet dependent.** In today's communication environment, asking field sales to "hook up" whenever they need to access their data or even use their software reflects disrespect for sales

---

[12] "Web Computing Stinks," John C. Dvorak, *PC Magazine*, December 1, 1999.

and detachment from reality. In most CRM environments, field sales needs access to data on the spot. The fact that it's hours-old data versus real time data doesn't matter as much as having it. And sales needs to do more than look at its data: it needs to work it with CRM software.

Yes, we all know that sooner or later wireless data communication will be available enough, reliable enough and fast enough to give us instant access to internal or external websites wherever and whenever. But we knew that ten years ago, too. And when wireless finally arrives as our primary remote data access tool, guess what? CRM users will be able to bypass the Internet completely and go *directly* wherever they want. In other words, the increasingly available "go anywhere" wireless phone service is the forerunner of direct, point-to-point data communication that may obviate the Internet for business-to-business, CRM purposes. More on this last point in the next chapter.

- **"CRM" is a three-letter word. It's customer relationship management, not customer management.** When I hear CRM described as the controls that run e-commerce, I want to puke. Transactional business is transactional business is transactional business—whether it happens over the Net, in stores, by mail, by phone or through caveside barter. And guess what. Customers don't *want* relationships with everyone they buy from.

Hey, let's get real about this last bit. Think about all the products and services you touch in a day. You wake up lying on a branded mattress and branded sheets. You turn off a branded alarm clock. You get ready with branded soap, toothpaste, toilet paper, shaving stuff or makeup (or maybe both), after-shave or fragrance (same stuff, different bottles), plumbing fixtures, towels and on and on. Then you sit down to a branded bowl of branded cereal with branded milk and fruit with branded coffee, a newspaper and maybe a branded smoke. Then you open your branded door, open your branded garage door with a branded opener, plop down in your branded car (which runs on branded gas, oil and anti-freeze here in Minnesota). And it doesn't stop when you get to work or have lunch or eat dinner or do anything with your kids. Oh, clothes, I just sent you out naked. How could I forget branded clothes. One brand for every body part for every gender for every age group. And we've still got recreation, lawn care, stuff to read, stuff to sit on.

> **Customer relationship management, the CRM stuff, applies only to relationships that customers want to have with sellers.**

Now, do you want to have a *relationship* with each and every seller of this stuff and each and every outlet that sells it? If you do, get a life. No, of course you don't. If these relationships are by e-mail, you'll load some buggy software and freeze your computer—for good. If it's by mail, you'll nail your mail box shut. By phone? You'll rip the damn thing off the wall. And in person? You'll "go postal." Over the Internet? You'll just stop going there. Boy, makes those caves sound awfully good.

So let's make a critical distinction here. Customer *relationship* management, the CRM stuff, applies only to relationships that customers want to have with sellers. Managing relationships that customers don't want but sellers do, that's good ol' push marketing and foot-in-the-back selling that's got nothing to do with CRM. In fact, it's antithetical to CRM and CRM values.

And that, folks, is the biggest reason why CRM does *not* equal e.com. No matter what the majority of marketing automation folks try to tell you. What these dressed up database marketers are selling is traditional, speak but can't hear, database marketing that customers are sick of—*upchuck* sick. *Capiche?*

Oh, and one more little note. Remember how I've already railed (and will do again) at database marketers claiming CRM as part of their schtick? Well, turnaround is not fair play. CRMers trying to lay claim to all of e-commerce are just as guilty—or guiltier, because they're supposedly smarter than database marketers.

Misunderstanding #3: It's Time to Get Out of Sync

Reading this chapter is going to feel like jumping into a bathtub of ice cubes (but a branded bathtub). Unfortunately, we've got to head back to the technology thicket—only this time we're going hip deep instead of ankle deep. And this time, I hope IT readers will hang in there and read—because what follows is not about sugar-coating or oversimplifying stuff. The issue at hand—replacing remote data synchronization with browser access to web-based databases and software—needs more of your attention than the passing comments made so far. We need to drill down on the issues so you fully understand the argument and what's at stake for you.

Once upon a time, way back about two years ago, *remote data synchronization* was the accepted way of coordinating field data with a central CRM database, which usually resided at corporate HQ. Hell, it was the only way. And for a long time, synchronization had seemed the very soul of first SFA, then CRM. But when more and more of us started sticking the web needle in our arms and overdosing, many started believing that web-based CRM technology could and would do away with synchronization completely.

So now we're threatening to abandon synchronization. We're leaving her for the siren song of web-based databases. Hey, who needs all the mess and complexity of data synchronization? Most companies with field sales forces that are implementing CRM need it, but that hardly seems the point.

Many of us started sticking the web needle in our arms and overdosing.

Making everyone access one customer database via web-browser seems like such an elegantly simple solution. Fire up. Connect to our web-server. Do what work you need to do. See what information you need to see. *Voila! Trés facile.* Slam dunk. Who could argue with that? Well, maybe some counter-revolutionaries who still believe in empowering salespeople by putting customer data where it does the most good—at the point of customer contact.

And whatever could we have been thinking about anyway, messing around with something so *in*elegant as remote data synchronization? And what the heck is it, anyway? Even though it's being eclipsed by the wonderful webness of web, we should at least describe what it is—if only to plan what we should put on its tombstone.

Now, it's hard to talk about remote data synchronization without confusing the daylights out of non-technical people. Or boring half-to-death the plastic pocket-liner contingent. It's so complex, yet so mundane. But I'll try to find a happy medium or at least a mutually unhappy medium.

Remote data synchronization is a fancy term for simultaneous exchange of new or changed data among non-networked computers (which ain't too shabby an expression itself). Let's try that again. Data synchronization means swapping data between only intermittently networked computers running the same sales automation software in order to keep everyone running on the same data. The *same software* stipulation will soon fall, but it's still a limitation right now.

Okay, to sum it up, remote data synchronization permits multiple users running the same CRM software on their not-always-networked computers, usually laptops, to exchange data back and forth so the CRM system user has the latest and greatest information.

And how, pray tell, does this miracle called "synchronization" actually occur?

Here's how. Synchronization of more than two computers relies on two elements.

1. A reference database housed on a central computer, which keeps the true facts, or at least the latest. Sales automation types often refer to this central computer as "the server"—although often it's not a true server, in IT-speak.

2. Communication links established between the sales automation server and remote users.

When that server is housed at corporate HQ and all remote users dutifully synchronize directly with the server – that's,

One-step or WAN (wide area network) synchronization.

Remote users temporarily connect to the WAN to synchronize, then leave the network until the next time they want to synchronize. Different from accessing one web database with a browser because now we have *multiple databases*—field databases and the server database—that we have to keep current.

But if there's "one-step" synchronization, you're probably guessing that "two-step" synchronization comes next, and we're going to discuss it. Unfortunately, especially if you're struggling to stay awake right now, you're right. Lots of those pesky customers who bug the daylights out of software developers keep yearning for old-fashioned,

Two-step or LAN (local area network) synchronization.

Talk about messy. In two-step synchronization, individual remote users synchronize with a database housed on a field server at their local or regional office. That server, in turn, synchronizes with the ultimate database housed on the central server, back at corporate HQ. Great theory, although much harder from a technology standpoint—and not as fashionable as using WANs. But "harder" isn't always bad—especially when using WAN synchronization in CRM often means dumping giant vats of data into those sink holes euphemistically called "data warehouses"—instead of the much more efficient and economical method of keeping data where it's used most, which two-step, LAN synchronization does best. Besides, new database technologies are taking much of the pain out of two-step synchronization.

But enough about "one-step two-step" stuff. To avoid confusion, let's just remember them as "WAN-sync" for one-step and "LAN-sync" for two-step. *Simplement?*

WAN-sync

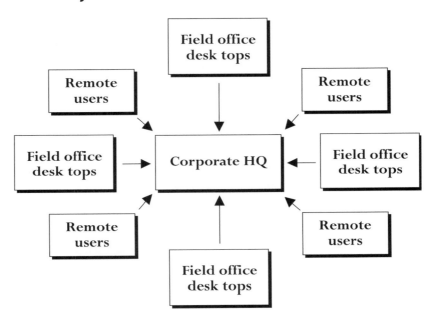

WAN-sync (one-step synchronization),
all data passes through a single hub

LAN-sync

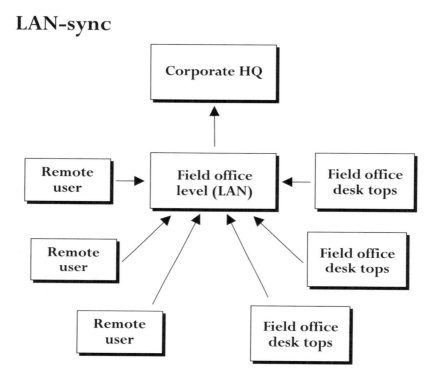

With LAN-sync (two-step synchronization), data synchronization occurs at both regional and enterprise levels.

Okay, now we've got a head of steam going. On to the rest of synchronization. Aside from choosing between WAN-sync and LAN-sync, synchronizing sales automation users also have to select among several different methods of communicating among computers. Originally, a plain old modem-to-modem connection over standard telephone lines was the connection of choice. Dial up the regional or central computer. Synchronize. Disconnect. See you later. You pay the phone bill. But modem connections are *passé*, at least in some circles. Today, we've got jazzier options. Like synchronizing *over* the web to our reference database on the corporate server. We can even use e-mail and exchange synchronization files in mail boxes, handy as all get out. And for the really forward thinkers among us, we can dispense with the wireline telephone service entirely and digital cellular or the data-only wireless service becoming available in major metro markets. But we've already opened that can of worms.

'Nuff of that. Now we're done with synchronization. Big head stone, eh? No wonder we're getting out of sync. And it sure seems the web can do everything synchronization can do and more, right?

Wrong. Wrong. Wrong. Those darned appearances. They get so deceitful.

Let's ask a dumb question. For *whom* is the web solution so much simpler? And I'll sneak in one more. For *whom* is most CRM technology designed?

You could be a cynic and answer the second question, "Of course it's designed for IT, just like every other information system in the company." Which of course answers the first question as well.

But let's not be cynical. Instead, let's ask yet another question. "Isn't CRM supposed to change the behavior of an *internal* customer base?" Most of all, our sales people? Sure is. But here's the catch. We in the CRM industry get so blinded so often by the wonders of technology that we forget about not only our external customers, but our internal customers as well—those poor blokes on the other end of our fancy, web-this or web-that systems.

Let's think for a minute about what the web option means to *them*—to those sales people who have to use these elegant web-based solutions.

A good place to start these thoughts is with a fresh and original concept:

A chain is only as strong as its weakest link.

Glad I thought that up. So now let's look at this chain involving your choice of using either synchronization or a single web-based database to enable field sales to keep their data (and everyone else's) current. One link (or process step) at a time, from the salesperson's perspective, here we go.

1. Find a phone.

2. Call up some ethereal entity that's supposed to ask you where you want to go today.

3. They have to answer your call.

4. If there's an answer, you can ask to go to wherever your server database lives.

5. Your database has to accept your call.

6. You give your database any new data you've gathered.

7. Then, if you're synchronizing, you get back any updates for the customer records you manage. If you're on a browser accessing your web-based database, you can ask to see anything you're cleared by security to see.

8. Finally, if you're synchronizing, you log off and walk away with a full set of data on your customers. If you're "browsing," you walk away with a nearly empty laptop computer (easier to carry without all that data).

Now, would someone please identify one link in this chain that's *strengthened* by using a single, web-based database and accessing it through a browser—rather than synchronizing between field-level and server databases, the old-fashioned way? Speak up! Well—I'll break this deafening silence and identify three links that are *weakened* by web databases: 1) funneling every call over an Internet "system" that still lacks bandwidth—an invitation for bottlenecks to occur; 2) forcing sales people to access the web every time they want to do anything, which discourages using the system at all; and 3) sending sales the message that big brother must tell them what to do with their data, not exactly motivational or empowering.

And would someone please identify which *sales* problems the web-based database address (other than learning sales automation software rather than a simple-minded browser)? No answer? Well, let's discuss two problems Web-based databases *don't* address.

1. **Finding a phone.** We don't update field data as often as we should because we can't call in. Of course, we can always unplug the customer's lobby phone and do it there. Good way to get a forearm shiver to the face from the friendly receptionist—the one with deep jowls. And if we do escape the corporate guard dog's watchful eyes, we're liable to smell burning the moment we attempt to activate that hard-wired, inconvenient and expensive-to-replace internal modem through the lethal enterprise telephony switch. Smoke leaking from every notebook orifice. Springs and other small parts leaping out of what once was our screen. You name it. Do you like your modems over easy or sunny-side up?

   And we all know that wireless data transmission ain't yet ready for prime time.

2. **Having all our data where and when we need it.** If you're in sales, you don't need an explanation of the value of having all your data with you all the time, versus accessing your browser and downloading a few files at a time. I know that

because whenever I present to sales groups, I talk about "getting chopped off at the knees" after walking blind into a horrible billing or service or delivery problem. I invariably get knowing nods from almost everyone. That's why sales gets hazard pay. That's why the golf clubs and fishing rods ride around in so many sales car trunks. For recovery time after our best account commits surgery on us.

And one more thing. If we expect our salespeople to become information-driven, let's give them the doggone information! They need to work *all* their customer data offline in order to respond to data, find opportunities in it, take responsibility for it. But that's the way we so often are with sales. Tell 'em to do something then take away the tools they need.

Before we start abandoning synchronization for that web stuff, we'd better take a closer look at *what* we are supposed to be doing with CRM data and *why*. If we keep our focus where it should be—on improving customer relationships and improving customer-related work processes—we'll be much less likely to get out of sync.

Misunderstanding #4:
It Will Be Over In a Quarter
(And You Won't Feel a Thing)

Hey, the race is on. Which sales automation software system can implement the fastest? Lotsa software sellers are anxiously gunning their engines, ready to zip through the entire sales automation implementation course at warp speed. Their get-it-done-now clients, unfazed by the risks of speed, are poised to drop their starting flags. Ready, set, go…crash#@&*slam##%^(!!!

What a mess. Pedal to the metal quickly ends in metal on metal and metal against anything else in sight. Wrecked CRM projects litter the track. Many more have already left the track. And those that miraculously negotiate the deadly turns emerge dented beyond recognition—fit only for the junkyard where dead projects wither away. May they rust in peace. Amen.

Some paranoids might think some sinister force is crouched behind the retaining walls at every turn of the implementation track, dousing each bend with oil while we're focused on the speeding projects racing towards us. Who would be perverse enough to do such a terrible thing? Someone who's got it in for software vendors?

Okay. Enough fantasy. Someone reasonably balanced seeing this mess—especially someone who's been around the track more than once—would figure this one out right away. Chalk up this demolition derby to CRM being inherently slippery. Too damn slippery to negotiate at high speed. Not to mention too populated with axle-breaking potholes; cul-de-sacs masquerading as short-cuts, and neon signs luring us to *turn right for web-based, turn right for web-based.* Too bad there's only a dirt road at the end of that web off-ramp. And don't those software drivers steering these rapid implementation projects remember the old Indy slogan, "Go fast, turn *left,* go fast turn *left.*" But hey, we're an industry of pioneers and rule breakers, aren't we?

> **Fortunately, not everyone drives the CRM track like a maniac.**

Fortunately, not everyone drives the CRM track like a maniac. Smart drivers, the ones who live to drive another day, know it's a long race. They know you'd better learn the track, backwards and forwards, before running it. And they're smart enough to know that every track is different. Want to tell me you can implement CRM in my company in 90 days—without knowing anything more than what your product can do (and can't)? Watch me run from you, faster than any racecar you've ever seen.

And by the way—what is the big rush?

Guy named John Ulrich, while he was running Target Stores, made a trendy business credo out of the phrase, *Speed is life.* Great stuff if you happen to be retailing fashion, trendy toys or other fads. But who was that "Barney" character, anyhow? And are trouser cuffs *gauche* or *de rigeur* this season?

What does discount retailing have to do with CRM? Nothing. Then why imitate retail business practices by trying to implement at warp speed serious, complex and supposedly last-ing stuff like CRM?

Guess we have our reasons. The fact that rapid deployment even exists in CRM proves that we can, if we close our eyes, make a *cogent* sounding case for these "jam jobs." Cogent if we don't object to more than a little disingenuous rationalization. Too bad the case for rapid implementation of CRM breaks down under the slightest scrutiny. Look just below the quasi-logic for implementing CRM at breakneck speed and you can see the trouble coming. But hey, who has time to look?

> **Rushing a disruptive CRM system out the door takes everyone's eyes off the customer.**

Not to push this all on soft-ware sellers, though. Many of their customers are all to eager to believe they can just jam CRM through without any kind of adverse outcomes. Why not? All we're doing is adopting new customer strategies that…you know the rest. No prob-lem. No, *big* problem. You'd think we'd think twice and think again before changing strategies, activities and processes like we're changing clothes. But hey, who has time to think?

"We have to hurry to keep pace with change" is one ratio-nale for gunning it. But that's the mantra of the new millennium. And of course we have to keep pace with change in our hyper-competitive markets. But let's remember the tor-toise and the hare. The race to implement CRM is a lot like their race. Slow and steady gets there first. Old and trite? The more things change, the more they stay the same.

"We can't afford to keep selling this way," is another flimsy reason given for shotgun CRM. But think about it this way. Can you afford to virtually *stop* selling while attempting to force through a CRM implementation—only to find yourself imple-menting again and again and again because you didn't get it right the first time? Worse than not getting it right, these jam jobs are highly likely to get things horribly wrong.

"We're losing opportunity by the day." That's a good one. May also be true. But would you rather temporarily lose opportunity or risk permanently losing what you have already? Rushing a disruptive CRM system out the door takes everyone's eyes off guess who? The customer. Customers don't like that. And they often voice their displeasure with their feet. Of course, we could pretend that implementing our new CRM system won't be disruptive. But that goes hand-in-hand with pretending we're doing CRM. CRM is only successful when it disrupts old functional activities and work processes and replaces them with more customer-centric perspective stuff. And guess what? The more disruption, the better job you may be doing.

"We practice 'fast fail.'" Oh, gosh. That's my favorite. We've developed a few other slogans to express the same inanity: "Analysis, paralysis." "Let the market decide." "Real-time development." Cute. Too bad they're all ways of expressing aversion to planning. "Takes too long." "We don't have the time." "Things never work out the way we planned." They don't? Then learn how to plan.

Implementing CRM without an adult dose of pre-implementation planning—covering business strategy, sales and service integration, sales and marketing integration, process re-engineering, culture change, organizational change and, oh yes, technology—is a one way ticket to that junkyard of dead projects. Go directly to the project graveyard. Do not pass "Go."

But sales hype from some software companies and overeager clients notwithstanding, wouldn't you think common sense alone would stop us from jumping into rapid deployment CRM? Guess we're trying to prove Horace Greeley was right when he said, "Common sense is uncommon." Or at least trying to prove he wasn't wrong. But now comes the really scary part. You don't even have to rely on our common sense. All you have to do is walk across the office into the back room and ask what *they've* experienced with rapid implementation of ERP[13] systems. Boy, will you get an earful.

And consider this. Implementing ERP is far *less* disruptive than implementing CRM. Yes, ERP does involve major changes, but at the process level, not the strategic or functional activity levels. ERP doesn't change worldviews like CRM does. It does what we're already doing better. That's not so hard to swallow. Sure, a few functional changes may be required. But ERP doesn't threaten the existence of whole departments or radically change reporting lines. CRM, done right, can do that. Hey, why not just waltz into marketing and explain that a big chunk of their ad budget will now go to customer information management? Or drop by accounting and tell them that customer service is moving to the front-office system and will henceforth

> **Why not just waltz into marketing and explain that a big chunk of their ad budget will now go to customer information management?**

be joined with sales? Or fly out to greet distributors with the news that you'll be communicating directly with their customers that buy your products through them. You won't need a plane to fly back.

Furthermore, the back-office folks work with much more predictable processes. They don't have to contend with those squirrelly little critters called "customers"—who seem to delight in doing the opposite of what we expect at the time we least expect it. So big shot ERP vendor's system can come complete with pre-programmed processes and get away with it. Try

---

[13] For readers not acquainted with "ERP," it stands for "enterprise resource planning." That's a fancy way of describing managing manufacturing and operations.

that in the front office. These nicely pre-programmed processes, developed without specific knowledge of your customers' buying cycles or idiosyncrasies, are more likely to blow up in your face than work. Which is why CRM is never going to work as a forward extension of ERP. Why would anyone think it would?

Hey, if the back-office folks can't deploy ERP rapidly, what are we thinking when we try to jam CRM through in 90 days?

I'll tell you one thing we're *not* thinking about—the impact on customer contact people most affected by CRM. It's that same common thread in CRM that pops up to bite us you-know-where more often than we care to admit—at work again. *The people CRM affects most matter least.* We're often not concerned about CRM's impact on the salespeople and service people affected most. "Those whining salespeople have it coming to them." "Service people are expendable and easy to replace." Etc., etc., etc.

Bonus hint here. When you're selecting CRM software, look carefully at each vendor's promotional materials. Really read this stuff. You'll get lots of dim views of sales and service people. "Hey, we're the big stick that's gonna whip those slackers into shape." Yeah, right.

Discouraging, eh? But, rapid deployment CRM is a classic expression of our disdain for "lowly" customer-contact people. Far from the only such expression, but we can only address one slight at a time. *N'est pas?* And don't forget to drive with the brakes on.

Misunderstanding #5:
CRM = Database Marketing
(Otherwise Known as "The Big Lie")

Thought we already killed this dead horse, too? Nah. Or should I say "neigh." It's like chopping arms off a giant octopus (if I'm right and they do just grow back new tentacles). Just can't kill it. So we'll wound it some more.

Three things are more likely to screw up CRM than anything else. Confusing it with software is *numero uno.* Failing to garner proactive top management support is number two. And confusing CRM with database or direct or whatever-the-heck-we-want-to-call-it marketing is number three—and contending for a higher position on the list. Sure, CRM functional activities on occasion include direct mail, telemarketing and stuff like that. But CRM is so much bigger than that. Orders of magnitude bigger. Which begs the question, why the confusion?

Because we're human, for openers. We all share a human tendency to slot new things—like CRM— into familiar reference frameworks. Among all the marketing truths I tried over the years to impart to the graduate students in my database marketing and micro-marketing courses, the tendency of customers to "slot" a new product category into an established brain compartment ranks right at the top in importance. That's how we understand something new. By comparing it to what we know. *Ergo,* people coming face to face with CRM for the first time tend to compare CRM to direct marketing and especially "database marketing," the computer component of direct marketing. Hey, we get that stuff without having to read books about it.

But there's more to the confusion than the way we think.

We all share a human tendency to slot new things—like CRM— into familiar reference frameworks.

There's a huge mother industry out there—direct/database marketing—which desperately wants to lay claim to CRM as their own new wrinkle. A tactic trying to own a strategy. At trade conferences, in trade publications, in trade meetings, in all of the places we learn about what's new and what's happening in marketing (as opposed to sales), direct marketers have been misrepresenting CRM as a component of their craft; a by-product of their industry, a part of their revenues (which they try to inflate more than advertising inflates its revenues, to see who's top dog in the traditional marketing income race). And when that wasn't working so well, they pulled an "if you can't beat 'em, join 'em" move and came up with a concept called "marketing automation." Get it? Sales automation, service automation, so *marketing* automation. Despite the fact that most of what's called marketing automation is database marketing in disguise—not CRM. Just old worms in new cans.

That's the big lie. That CRM fits into and even under database marketing.

It took me an embarrassingly long time to understand why the direct marketing industry so persistently scales down CRM to fit its toolboxes. But finally, I got it. I was attending a database marketing conference in Orlando several years ago when I had my own, personal epiphany. Or, better yet, the devil appeared and flashed his horns before me.

Let's replay some of the low lights of this conference—which were *low* enough to sneak under my thick skull and produce a blinding flash of the obvious. In my defense, "the obvious" is often what's most difficult to see—witness our readiness to accept as part of CRM all of what the database dudes are calling "marketing automation."

But on with the story. 'Tis always a pleasure to skip out of ice-box-cold Minnesota in winter for points south. So I was looking forward to attending this deal, which just happened to be in December. The meeting's sponsors bill this event as a twice-yearly summit of the database marketing industry. I had gone once before. But even though I was still doing some database marketing-type stuff, I had waited three years to go again. That seemed about the right time—given the relatively slow rate of change in the database marketing biz.

Now, I admit that I let my expectations rise a little high. Okay, very high. But not without reason. The scheduled keynote speakers were Don Peppers and Martha Rogers. The closing-day general session featured Clifford Stoll of *Silicon Snake Oil*[14] fame, a harsh critic of *substituting* computer relationships for personal ones, rather than using their combined power. Both one-to-one marketing, which Peppers and Rogers espouse, and building personal buyer-seller relationships have long been part of my belief system—since the early 1980s, when I switched over from sales to marketing. So Orlando seemed like the right place to be. Especially because I was still trying, unsuccessfully, to rec-

---

[14] Clifford Stoll, *Silicon Snake Oil: Second Thoughts on the Information Highway* (New York: Anchor Books, 1995).

oncile developing customer relationships with database marketing. Couldn't find the fit. But it had to be there, no?

Beyond the featured speakers and the normal tracks of normally boring sessions, the conference also offered a day of pre-conference intensives that caught my attention. Hey, these sessions might provide an opportunity to figure this stuff out.

And beyond the specific events, there was change in the air. That's what really motivated me to go, aside from the weather. The whole business of applying customer information to aid the marketing process was undergoing a metamorphosis. Hey, we had a shift from corporate use of marketing data to field use of customer data; another shift from using indirect and inferred knowledge of customers to direct knowledge captured at the point of customer contact; a transition from using information to support centralized direct mail and telemarketing programs to applying information at the point of customer contact to build relationships; and even the stirrings of accepting of sales, service and marketing as interrelated processes. All this way back in 1996, when this shindig occurred.

I wanted to see how the database marketing industry would address change. And foolish me, I actually expected that the conference would address stuff such as:

Customer information becoming the ultimate competitive weapon—especially for organizations marketing to high-lifetime-value customers. With product parity becoming more the rule than the exception, even in high tech and big ticket markets, managing customer information was becoming the critical point of distinction that separates winners from losers. Just like product superiority used to determine success, once upon a time, not many years ago. Much more exciting stuff than finetuning mailing list scoring techniques, ugh! Or 15 new variants of good ol' merge-purge, yuk!

CRM (we still called it SFA) arriving full force—changing the way we dealt with high value customers. Some of us were already melding sales and service data to arm customer contact folks with real knowledge. As opposed to data assembled, processed and stored at the corporate level, then doled out to the *peons* in the field.

Relationship marketing (or one-to-one marketing, if you prefer) becoming a reality—and not a Peppers and Rogers' prediction. "Mass customization" was becoming more than a catchy phrase. Not to mention that product development driven by direct customer input, rather than product management projections, was on the scene. Hey, what an opportunity for everyone involved in customer information management!

Distributed data management had finally arrived—better late than never. Marketing was years behind other disciplines in intelligently deploying data at appropriate levels. The marketing data gurus were constrained by fear of data misuse by generalists untrained in database marketing, not to mention the "lepers" in field sales. Boy, did field sales take some hits to their character during this conference.

As it happened, session attendees did raise questions regarding how to work effectively with field sales in customer data collection and management. But their questions—even insistent questions—got buzzed off.

So what's my problem, anyway? You don't have to be a bleeding heart to hear the steam hissing out of my ears. You probably suspect that the Orlando conference really stuck in my craw. And you know what? You're right. I felt like Andy Rooney on a really bad day. Maybe I went to the wrong conference. But how could that be? Peppers and Rogers talking about customer relationships, Stoll talking about trashing customer relationships if we misuse the Internet, fellow travelers, how could I not belong there?

But I sure didn't belong in most of the sessions I attended. Get this. The pre-conference intensive I attended turned out to be a history lesson. The speaker fessed up that his slides were several years old. They must have been, because they were filled with the names of dead soldier companies already buried by change, and even included, by the speaker's admission, dead or dying service categories obviated by market changes.

Also during this session, that nasty issue of sales involvement in database marketing popped up during Q&A. This "expert" sidestepped it several times. I couldn't stop asking myself, "How can an expert in database marketing ignore that sales and marketing are joined at the hip?" What was this guy, retro?

After the session, during which I contributed several uncharacteristically polite remarks about different approaches used in building customer databases versus marketing databases, the marketing director for one of this country's better-known financial service providers followed me out of the room. Actually, he chased me. He was hot. He cornered me and started yelling about why this conference and these presenters didn't get it about salespeople being indispensable in building customer relationships. Good thing it was before lunch, so he didn't have garlic breath. I empathized with him and agreed with him (good thing, too, because he was one big guy). But I still didn't get it…about what was going down at this conference.

So I attended an afternoon intensive session that was samo, samo. This clown actually waved off the customer relationship management movement as a blip on the screen—just another source of data to be rolled up into the traditional direct mail database. Yeah, he made the obligatory references to needing to get beyond a myopic focus on what he termed "centers of tactical excellence." But he then spent the remaining two and a half hours of his session doing database segmentation from the old days. I wanted to ask this new version of the morning's presenter, "When are you coming out of hibernation?" What restraint on my part, eh?

Day two. The regular conference day got off to a better start. Peppers and Rogers spoke. Sure, I used to jokingly tell my students that the authors must have been smoking rope when they wrote the last several chapters of *The One to One Future*—that's how hypothetical they get. But together, they've contributed lots to CRM from the marketing side. Probably more than anyone else. But even their presentation was troubling. Troubling because they were introduced as part of the database marketing family and somehow symbolic of the conference. No kidding, *somehow*. Their presentation was antithetical to damned near everything else I saw and heard at the conference, except for Stoll and the attendees who kept asking questions about customer-contact stuff and not getting answers.

But get this. After proclaiming from their lecterns that most everything I'd witnessed in the pre-conference sessions and about everything I'd hear in subsequent sessions was off base, Peppers and Rogers got a thunderous round of applause. Hey, some people hear what they want to hear. Make that lots of people.

Peppers' and Rogers' presentation was antithetical to damned near everything else I saw and heard at the conference.

But as the conference wore on, it became more and more apparent that a lot of other folks who listened were turned off by most of what they heard. The conference was supposed to be about the future. What it was really about was the past. I saw streams of attendees leaving sessions early, with distressed expressions on their faces. Caught some grumblings like, "Just the same old stuff." "Who picked that panel?" "Why won't they address sales issues?" And best of all, "Would somebody tell that joker there's more to life than house file, merge-purge; house file, merge-purge?"

But there was more to come. Cute stuff like, "There's one thing we have to understand, you can't trust customers, they lie." "We already have too much customer information." "You can't start a database with customer information, you have to define your segments first." "You should spend at least two hours with a client before designing their SFA database." "We have an interactive dialog with our customers once a month [a credit card marketer referring to their statement]." But the capper for me was a rhetorical question asked by one presenter: "This Peppers and Rogers stuff is fine, but does anyone here really market one-to-one?" I raised my hand, ready to carve him into little pieces, but he kept right on blathering, "No, of course you don't, it's impractical, so let's talk about customers in segments of at least a thousand." I got up and left. Better than dismembering this clown, limb by limb (verbally, of course).

> **This conference wanted to publicly embrace all the emerging CRM stuff and claim all of it as part of database marketing.**

In fact, the only remaining point of interest for me (at least in the positive sense) was Stoll's presentation. Without my glasses, I could mistake this guy for Robin Williams. Stoll provided some comic relief for an otherwise dreary event. He was focusing primarily on the Internet, but virtually everything he expressed concern over applied equally to traditional database marketing. Reducing customers to a name, a customer number, a segmentation code and a mishmash of inferred or applied data (in other words, educated guesses) inhibits, rather than fosters, customer dialog and customer intimacy.

Stoll, too, received enthusiastic applause. Must have been for his humor.

Gee, what happened? As disheartening as the content of the conference turned out to be, the conference dynamics were worse. From a distance you could mistake the sink hole between the views of the featured speakers and those of the conference presenters for accommodating, "big tent" stuff. And you could write off the probing questions of attendees that went ignored, because that's not what this conference wanted to be about. But not if you were there, you couldn't. This conference wanted to publicly embrace Peppers and Rogers' one-to-one approach to marketing and all the emerging CRM stuff, borrow the luster and, of course, claim all of it as part of *database marketing.*

But inside the sessions—where the real conference took place—the talk was of segmentation, scoring and mass number crunching, and how to improve direct mail results and justify even more direct mail. All *what* data and no *why* knowledge. An attitude you'll detect if you look below the veneer of most "marketing automation" stuff.

I'm truly embarrassed to confess how long it took me to get it. But I've talked to others with database marketing backgrounds similar to mine who also persisted in trying to connect what they used to do (to some degree), database marketing, with what they do now, CRM—until they experienced their own blinding flash of the obvious.

On the morning of the third and last day, while I was sitting and stewing over a coffee, somebody turned the light on. I felt like a jerk. What the hell was I expecting? The database marketing industry doesn't want to change. It can't afford to. Sure it wants to look current, but...

All of a sudden I was flooded by memories of, get this, the stir Dwight Eisenhower made with his parting speech as President—the one where he took on the military-industrial complex, warning us that we could not and should not determine defense policy by the machinery and skills we have in place to build armaments. That was the cart leading the horse. Instead, Ike had maintained, we must adapt our skills and machinery to meet our needs. Okay, I was in junior high school at the time, but my folks talked a lot about politics, and I overheard this stuff.

Ike's analogy about production capacity driving solutions applied directly to the database marketing industry. Applies even more today.

Information-based marketing had divided into two industries: database communication and what was to become customer relationship management.

This industry is hugely vested in the machinery and skills required to pump out high volumes of direct mail and huge numbers of telemarketing calls—as productively as machines will allow. That and big-butt computers to figure out where to fire messages—whether by postal mail, e-mail, semi-automatic, whatever. But this stuff doesn't work well for acquiring and managing customer data at the customer contact level. For that matter, it doesn't work at all. Same for the human skills. The ears lose their sensitivity if you spend much time hugging web presses and machine inserters.

It occurred to me later (much later than it might have occurred to other people) that I had totally retooled myself without realizing it—new toolbox, new skill set, new everything. I'd left the advertising/direct marketing agency business, and for the most part left database marketing, because I was spending the majority of my time doing the wrong things the wrong way—because I couldn't figure out how to practice the personal-level marketing I believed in while trapped in an agency environment, using traditional database marketing skills.

So that's what I was doing, on my own, consulting in what would soon be called "CRM."

But back to the conference. Instead of focusing on change, the conference had concerned itself with, how do we utilize our existing capacity? This conference was all about preserving a role for our present inventory of machinery and skills. It was, in that sense, a conference dedicated to resisting change, or slowing it down. Not a conference about embracing or even accepting change. Change was not an option.

Information-driven marketing had divided into two industries: *database communication* and what was to become *customer relationship management*. From a subject-matter standpoint, the conference made several forays beyond providing computer support for direct mail and telemarketing applications. But these came across as tokenism, as attempts to lay claim to the changes that were already overtaking the traditional database marketing industry. "Hey Dick, wake up. You're in competition with these guys." Which is exactly how I feel about three-quarters or more of the *marketing automation* stuff I see today.

Database marketing is competing with CRM for share of budget dollars, for share of jobs, for share of stature. In an ironic way, the competition resembles the age-old tug-of-war between database marketing and advertising. Database marketing made a lot of hay over claims that it was more personal, more customer-friendly than advertising. So guess what. Here I am writing about database marketing from the CRM perspective, just as database marketers wrote about advertising. The shoe is now on the other foot. What goes around comes around. Whatever. Guess that shows we all live in glass houses. Hope I haven't thrown too many big stones.

No big surprise, in hindsight, that relationship marketing and CRM don't mix with database marketing in one conference. Peppers and Rogers didn't belong at this conference. Nor did Stoll. Nor did a considerable number of people who attended.

That's why it really annoys me when traditional database marketers wave the CRM flag. Or climb inside a Trojan horse named "marketing automation." Or transport their tactics to the Internet and claim they're doing new stuff. Or when they run in front of CRM like little kids trying to get into the picture saying—"That CRM stuff, that's us."

No, that's not you. Not even close.

[Postscript: I'm in sunny Phoenix, in January, four years later, doing one last copy check before this puppy goes to editing. Why am I here? Yesterday afternoon I spoke at a CRM conference—and there's a blizzard back home, so I'm stuck here. What's the real conference fare? Mostly good old database marketing disguised as something new. "Hey old paradigm, wrap yourself up in Internet technology and you look pretty good." Until, that is, the speaker before me blows your cover by telling attendees that Peppers and Rogers' one-to-one marketing is just a minor adjustment to database marketing. Poor bastard. He didn't know what he was about to run into. Five minutes into my presentation I let him have it—humorously, of course—but with sarcasm dripping like sap off a maple tree. Pancaked him. What's changed in four years? The disguise. Oh, and one more thing. The audience. I had a stream of people thank me after I finished for setting the record (and this guy) straight. Folks are starting to catch on to this charade. But it ain't dead yet. So we gotta keep beating it 'til it is.]

Misunderstanding #6: CRM is Too Hard, Too Risky, Too Expensive

There's no free lunch, either. Hey, customers taking charge, the influx of new sales and marketing technologies, the Internet—this stuff isn't making business easier. No, what it's doing is creating opportunity for hard working, risk-taking visionaries who can see past the next quarter's financials, and as a result, can tackle opportunities as big and challenging as CRM. And those that can't? Well, someone else's opportunity is going to come at their expense.

So please don't misinterpret my "don'ts" and "nots" as a black flag telling you to stay off the CRM course. No way. They're yellow flags saying, "Slow down," "Be careful" and "Don't let anyone lure you off course." In fact, I'd describe the CRM situation as "Damned if you do it wrong, damned if you don't do it at all." And that means lots of opportunity for those who do CRM right.

And remember why we're doing CRM in the first place. Customers are flexing their muscles, and woe be to any business that won't let their customers "take the wheel." In that context, doesn't matter that CRM is hard work. In business today, sticking around is hard work. And CRM is part of sticking around.

Besides, done right, it's a blast.

III. CRM Strategy

The Team(s)

CRM is a team sport. You may opt to use one team to guide CRM implementation from stem to stern. You may use separate planning and deployment teams, with the baton passing from one to the other mid-course. I happen to prefer the *one team approach,* but with increasing representation from field staff as the process goes on. Regardless. Forewarned is forearmed. Pick your CRM team(s) very carefully, or risk facing serious consequences down line. Or, to cut to the quick, make damn sure you *have* a representative CRM team (or two)—not a closed group of autocratic decision-makers.

You'd be astonished at how many CRM projects are designed by a group of corporate managers and nefarious consultants sitting around a corporate conference room table with carafes of coffee and a sideboard of Danish. *Sans* team, not a representative from customer relationship management in sight, often not even a representative from field marketing—but they're ready and willing to dictate how the minions in the field who interact with customers do their jobs. How arrogant. How dumb.

But, based on what you've read so far, you won't be a bit surprised to read that most CRM initiatives designed by corporate management and consultants—in isolation from customer relationship managers in sales and service and marketing—fail miserably. Ditto for those designed by eager-for-the-sale software vendors, who usually work in cahoots with IT departments that "know what's good for sales in particular and everyone else with customer contact."

Most CRM initiatives designed by corporate management and consultants—in isolation from customer relationship managers in sales and service and marketing—fail miserably.

Why do these "top-down" initiatives fail? Simple. They're usually marginalized or outright rejected by the customer-contact level staff they should support. CRM operates at the customer-contact level, not the corporate level. For CRM to be successful, sales, service and even marketing staff have to use it. And you guessed it. Winning sales compliance is a big problem.

Try turning CRM into a conduit for corporate types to bulk-ship stuff to field sales, and field sales will turn their backs on it. Try turning sales people into "information pickers" responsible for feeding a hungry data warehouse, and they'll starve your warehouse. Try extracting other stuff from sales without giving them what *they* want from CRM, and they'll walk away from it. Try turning sales into guinea pigs for testing the latest whiz-bang technologies, and they'll pull the plug on it. And try *forcing* sales to use your corporate-designed CRM system. Good luck. Any system not designed by customer relationship managers, or without their significant input, won't likely be used to manage customer relationships—or anything else.

Let's start by assuming we're going to have one team. Hey, I'm writing. I get to choose. Next, let's break down this team's core roles.

- **Market planning.** Developing customer relationship strategies driven by customer preference rather than corporate desires.

- **Activity planning.** Deciding how functional roles and responsibilities will have to change in order to implement these strategies.

- **Process re-engineering.** Determining how work processes must change for staff and departments to carry out these new roles and responsibilities.

- **Migration management.** Figuring out how the organization is going to get from Point A to Point B—without armed insurrection from individuals and departments that don't like what's going on.

- **Technology development.** Building a set of technology requirements and settling on which CRM software system to buy or build—plus figuring out integration with back-office systems.

- **Rollout.** Coordinating everything from new process/technology implementation to development of training materials to defending the project against naysayers who don't believe senior management has the will to implement CRM over their objections (and they're all-to-frequently right).

Pretty formidable, eh? Nope. Not *pretty* formidable. *Doggone* formidable. Not the kind of stuff you assign to middle management and ask them to carry out. "Oh, by the way, send me status report every week so I can keep tabs on you guys down there." Hey, senior manager with CRM stars in your eyes, better get your butt in gear and get out front of this stuff—because without you at the helm it's gonna crash right into a brick wall of internal resistance.

So who do you think should participate?

First, let's call up a basic team concept. Most well selected teams have two levels—core team members, folks who need to be involved most of the time, and resource members who fade

> **Don't ever develop customer-centric strategies without active participation of all customer-facing functions.**

in and out as needed. This two-tier structure minimizes people's time wasted in meetings that don't directly concern them—which maximizes their availability and attention when they're needed. Good way to go about it.

Now, let's start forming our team with core members. How about the heads of sales, marketing and service? Do I hear, "Don't need sales and service to develop strategies?" Wanna bet? Don't ever develop customer-centric strategies without active participation of *all* customer-facing functions. And that means including at least one each, preferably two, respected field sales and customer service operatives with direct customer contact. Think that will whiz off Mr. or Ms. So-and-so who thinks sitting with sales and service reps is beneath their dignity? Too bad. Maybe elevating customers to top-rung in importance should elevate the perceived importance of those most responsible for taking care of customers.

So who's next? A *very* senior IT person, to be sure. After all, we're going to be using information management technology, which is their bailiwick. And even though CRM technology might be "freestanding," you're not going far with CRM without integrating front-office and back-office data—and for that, IT's cooperation is hardly optional. Besides, a whole lotta IT folks are actively looking to expand their horizons, become business-savvy, make technology the cart and business strategy the horse. Hey, IT as a whole is doing a much better job making the transition into a customer-centric environment than database marketing with its "data-centric" mind set.

Anyone else? Be careful here. Most of us, even those of us who do this stuff day in and day out, have a tendency to *underestimate* how many different business functions within the organization CRM will affect. Before closing off membership on the core team, make sure you don't need a representative from manufacturing, purchasing, accounting or another back-office function. And while we're thinking expansively, think about including a senior human resource (HR) manager. If CRM has the potential to torque your organization around a turn or three, you might very well want an HR exec on the core team—and if you don't go that route at first, don't hesitate to recruit one down the road if CRM starts menacing some boundary-conscious folks, especially ones that could derail the whole project.

Here's a recruiting checklist for your core CRM team. Those bolded are usually musts—not optional. But bear in mind also the nearly universal opinion of those expert in forming work teams. Keep your core team to eight members max. You can add lots more resource members and bring them into lots of meetings, even change core members at key transition times like switching from strategy to deployment. But cap it at eight.

Potential Core Team Members

- **Senior sales exec**

- **Field sales operative(s)**

- **Customer service manager**

- **Customer service operative(s)**

- **Senior marketing exec**

- **IT "heavy"**

- Manufacturing manager

- Purchasing manager

- Accounting manager

- HR exec (organizational development type)

Does that look a little top-heavy to you? It's not. The "top-heaviness" reflects the magnitude of the decisions CRM requires companies to make. And we're not talking about these few making all the decisions. No way. They're not in close enough contact with customers. Which is why you should have customer-contact members on the core team—and involve customer folks of the resource team early on, when you're formulating customer relationship strategies, as well as later on, when you're into the nuts and bolts.

So what about the resource team?

More field sales people and managers. And not necessarily your star performers, either, but dedicated individuals with only average sales skills. You want average performers because CRM will help them most. Hey, your star performers already have their own process and information management system in their head, on paper, somewhere. CRM won't help them much, except by automating administrative tasks to give them more face time with customers. The primary sales-side benefits of CRM go to average performers—especially the kind that are more willing than able, a description that often covers the majority of a sales force. You may want to include sales stars on the core team, to help define best practices you want lesser lights to emulate. But keep them off the resource team. And by the way, compensate any sales rep you pull from the field to help develop CRM. Being part of your CRM initiative should never cost commissioned sales people a nickel.

Keep your core team to eight members max.

Beyond sales, who should you pick? More customer service folks, obviously. They're often the most accurate voice of customers, and you bring them in whenever you need your finger on the customer pulse. Marketing? Sure. Bring in more for strategic planning—then bring 'em back when you start reformulating communication with customers. But skip intractable database marketers if you can, and died-in-the-wool media advertising types as well. CRM often undercuts traditional, promotional marketing communication venues and replaces them with more personal communication among people who know each other. And that does tend to upset database marketing and advertising devotees.

But let's tap back-office resources as well. The typical CRM project will require team participation from decision-makers in manufacturing, often purchasing, almost always accounting and often logistics. Base these team-involvement decisions on your particular project. And if you leave someone out, don't hesitate to invite them in, even belatedly. Oh, and I'll put in one more plug for HR involvement, if they're not already on the core team.

Anyone missing? What about the web master? Or the web designer? Or the marketing department's Internet guru? Okay, maybe the latter. But it's far more important to include the web *engineer* from IT whose involvement you'll need to establish CRM-related Internet, intranet and extranet communication up and down the line—extending out to customers. Bottom line—pre-CRM Internet marketing is likely to be more old worms in a new can. Better not to worry about tying into Internet marketing programs that violate the spirit of CRM by trying to do stuff to customers rather than *with* them.

One overall word of caution here—about both core and resource team members. *Don't willingly accept "surrogates."* Surrogate members are lower-level folks sent to represent someone who feels too important to attend team meetings—but still wants a say. It's the "You have my vote (but I reserve the right to reverse your vote after the fact)," syndrome. If realities of corporate life do require you to accept a surrogate or two, insist on these three tenets.

1. Surrogates *must* be authorized to make decisions and commitments without subsequent review by whomever they represent. None of that, "I can't be there, but I have to pass on anything decided," bologna.

2. No surrogates for senior managers opposed to CRM or highly resistant to change. That's an invitation to disaster.

3. No sales or service managers as surrogates for contact-level staff. They're too likely to focus on controlling their people rather than empowering them to work effectively with customers.

And who's going to enforce all this? Your first line of defense is your team leader—the person who's supposed to maintain objectivity and stay above the fray. Although not always practical, ideally the team leader will be someone other than the already-named core team members—perhaps even an outsider. Regardless of whether inside or outside, here's what to look for in a team leader.

Attributes of Good CRM Team Leader

- Respected by team members *and* by senior management

- Objective, without strong personal agenda

- Task-oriented and able to work through distractions

- Good negotiator

- Resistant to sales pressure (from software vendors)

- With vision and eyes toward the future

- Comfortable with technology

Quite an imposing list. Reinterpret these requirements into any of those "four quadrant" personality profiling tests—you'd have a "four-cornered" kind of person, which doesn't happen in real life except in the presence of extreme stress, depression or other mental affliction. But you take the best candidate you can get.

Are we done now? Hardly. Not unless you want your CRM team ambushed and massacred in a dark hallway by a perturbed division manager or burned at the stake by turf-minded departmental managers. Your team leader is only your first line of defense against miscreants trying to torpedo CRM (and they exist in almost every CRM implementation setting). Your ultimate line of defense, your ace in the hole, is someone called the "team sponsor." The team sponsor is (or should be) a muckety-muck who's part of the executive-level decision to become a customer-centric company in the first place—the very decision that precedes virtually every successful CRM project. Your sponsor might be your CEO or an executive VP or corporate management's designated "change agent" who operates with full executive backing to make major changes of the type that typically engender resistance. Regardless, this person needs the clout to remove any and all obstacles thrown in CRM's way, regardless of who throws them. That's not a middle manager. Not a department VP either. Your team sponsor has to be a bonafide heavy hitter.

Selection of a team sponsor, which often becomes self-selection by the appropriate person, may turn out to be the most important decision relative to CRM that someone in your organization will make. The right sponsor can make all the difference. Believe me. I've been around more than a few projects with the wrong sponsor—some of which were stopped dead in their tracks.

Your team sponsor has to be a bonafide heavy hitter.

Are we done now? Sort of. But seems like you need half the senior managers in the organization on your team, and these folks are in high demand. How do you compete for their time? You can try begging. Or whining. Or pestering. Or seizing their electronic calendar and locking everyone else out. But the best way to involve them is through your (hopefully) all-powerful sponsor.

While you're forming your team, your sponsor should be informing the organization-at-large that CRM is coming, which will change the organization's fundamental relationships with customers, which will forever alter who does what, which will screw up established work processes all over the place, which could wreak havoc in the organization. What your sponsor probably won't want to add, although it's so true, is how upsetting CRM will be to folks who don't like anybody messing with their status quo for any reason. But these folks will get upset on their own—and that's your secret recruiting method.

Let your sponsor inform the organization about the sweeping changes CRM brings—including changes outside of sales, service and marketing. The team members you're looking for will probably come running in order to protect their turf.

Now let's touch on a frequently touchy point in the life of a CRM team. You've established your customer relationship strategy, and now you're ready to address required changes in how functional areas and their folks work. About this time, you'll

> **Let your sponsor inform the organization about the sweeping changes CRM brings.**

probably bring in several new core team members, not to mention a gaggle of new resource team members—many of them heads of departments that CRM will affect. And now that every decision-maker seriously affected by CRM is on the team, in one room, with urns (not carafes) of coffee, and carts full (not sideboards) of Danish, you're ready to go—except for this touchy point. *You have to get everyone on the same page.* Not easy, when you have a turf war ready to break out if anyone sneezes too loudly. Or taps their foot to the wrong tune. But doable.

Here's a technique I've used successfully to bring the most cacophonous teams together into at least semi-harmonious groups. The innocuous and boring name for this process—data mapping—lulls most team members into complicity in doing something they wouldn't do if they knew they were doing it. Here's the drill.

Let everyone stuff their faces with coffee and rolls, then you grab a marker and go to the white board. With group input, start drawing a diagram of how customer information flows through the organization. Start with the time you first identify a customer or potential customer and continue until there's no reason to keep their record active. Include in your map every single information change linked to an individual customer—in any department or function, not just sales, service and marketing. Almost infallibly, you'll see data moving from place to place unnecessarily. Data moving from department to department "on foot," often literally. Redundant operations. Wasteful operations. Ludicrous operations. Even counter-productive ones. And lots of operations that are too customer-unfriendly to believe. Anyone on the team who doesn't wind up laughing will probably wind up crying. And you know what? You haven't just defined your customer data flow. You've defined how your company interacts with customers. And everyone on the team is going to want to change that—soon.

Now comes the fun part. Fixing it. And beyond that, taking advantage of the opportunity CRM represents to do stuff that absolutely delights your current customers and attracts new ones—and makes every customer, new and old, more valuable than they would be *sans* CRM.

And hey, if everyone on your team starts with an open mind, you can delay this "data mapping" until you're ready to define new work in detail, even make it the last step before re-engineering work processes. But don't hesitate to use it now if you have to.

New Customer Contract

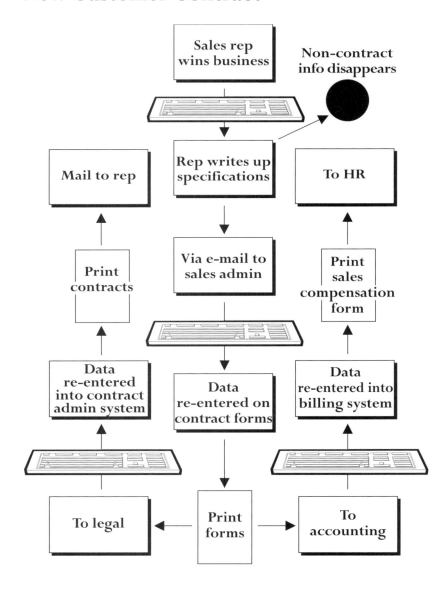

*This pictograph shows a tortuous route
to initiating a new customer contract.*

Customer Relationship Planning

Now that we've all had our little laugh about how we're interacting with customers and doing their business, it's time to wipe the grins off our faces—because we're headed straight into the soup. Hey, it's planning time. Time to determine what our relationships with customers should be. How we can make them "win-win" in the true meaning of that term. And how we should prioritize among what may be many opportunities to lengthen and strengthen customer ties.

Sounds great, except for one thing. Pardon me for being a little flip, but planning requires planning. It's the "P" word. Most business people are planning-averse in the extreme. No time to plan—but plenty of time to fail. No resources to commit to planning—but lots more resources available to sweep disappointment and defeat under the rug. Many of us outright hate planning. But most of us also hate failure. And staring at a 60% or 70% or whatever CRM failure rate just might make us regard planning as the lesser of two evils. And that doesn't mean doing "once over easy" planning, then sitting down to software demonstrations.

Early in my career, I saw more than enough train wrecks that originally passed for marketing strategies to forever warn me of the perils of casual, *ad hoc* planning. Sure, I've heard lots of "lightning bolt in the shower" stories about flashes of inspiration that saved the company. So have you. But for every supposedly successful strategy ignited by lightning, we can point to hundreds, thousands of fatal fires. Fact is, successful planning that leads to successful strategies more resembles rubbing together every possible combination of facts and perceptions until we set off a spark. Perspiration before inspiration.

Successful planning resembles rubbing together every possible combination of facts and perceptions until we set off a spark.

That's why, when I first set up shop as an agency market planner back in 1984, I sat down and painstakingly developed my own planning process. It's a process that requires gathering as much information as we can gather and working it, in a very specific sequence, as hard as necessary in order to set off that spark *through our own efforts*—rather than waiting for strategic inspiration to fall from the sky. It's hard work. But it does work. It worked back then. And thanks to the relative complexity of CRM compared to more traditional forms of marketing, it works even better today.

Over the years, this planning approach has produced many surprising outcomes—marketing approaches that went over, around and through "first obvious solutions" to create new opportunities. And many of these successful outcomes occurred addressing challenges that clients had already tried and failed to meet using traditional marketing approaches.

Why has it succeeded where other approaches failed? For two principal reasons. First, it's a full planning *process,* not glorified brainstorming or gimmick-driven "ideation" or the best we can come up with in a day's time at an off-site meeting. If you come from the marketing biz, you know the scene. Pull together a bunch of creative thinkers. Pull in the advertising agency. Describe the business issue in 25 words or less. Plunk down a big bowl of M&Ms smack in the center of a conference room table. Get sugar highs. Start bouncing off walls. Start shaking heads violently until two loose wires connect and set off a spark. Call that the "big idea." Call it a day. Pathetic. Doesn't work in a traditional marketing environment. Works worse in a CRM environment.

Hey, customers are complex creatures. CRM deals in their complexity. And planning that produces effective customer relationship strategies has to deal in their complexity—not to mention similarly complex channel considerations, competitive issues, perception-reality gaps, you name it. Want to figure this out over a bowl of M&Ms? Go do it for one of our competitors.

The second reason why this planning process works is that it flies in the face of the big-picture thinking of yesterday *and* today. Customer relationship planning forces us to shift focus from the mass audience to individual customers, from what makes customers similar to what makes them different, from customers do it one way (our way) to customers get it their way. Traditional marketing planning methods are top down—and in a CRM environment, you'd better be planning bottom-up. Seeing stuff at ground level, through lots of different customers' eyes, until we know how to satisfy as many customers as much as possible.

Hey, it's hard work. Damn hard work. But nowhere near as hard as the hard landings CRM implementations suffer when they start without a cogent customer relationship plan in place.

But back to the process itself, since its *trial run* with 3M Company back in the early 1980s, this "customer relationship planning process" has never stopped evolving. "Here's a better way to do this" experiences have driven some changes. Other, bigger changes have come in response to improved customer information acquisition and management capabilities (CRM technology especially), digital communication of many types (including the Internet), and the advent of automated process management in the sales environment—soon to go beyond the talk stage in the marketing environment. But the core elements—using planning to identify opportunities, rather than fulfill pre-determined objectives; listening to customers and those closest to them more than corporate execs furthest removed from customers; and emphasizing achieving share of customer over share of market—*the core elements remain unchanged.*

After keeping this process close to the vest for 15 years, I finally converted it into a guidebook and released it as *The Customer Relationship Management Planning Guide*—available on Amazon, our website *(www.h-ym.com)* and nowhere else. Hey, who's going to look for boring stuff like this in a bookstore?

In a nutshell, here's how this planning process flows.

- **Set a baseline.** Before you start planning, find out where you can go and where you can save yourself from making a long process even longer. For example, if you've maxed out production capacity on a particular product and can't readily ramp up, what's the point of persuading customers to buy more? Or, if customers really want you to go somewhere that capital restrictions put off limits, you may have to acknowledge to customers that you aren't going there soon. Hey, that's better than stringing them out.

- **Profile yourself.** If implementing CRM is likely to upset the organization and your CEO is change-averse in the extreme, maybe you need a job search more than a planning project.

- **Gather customer input—by the bucketful.** In a CRM environment, the customer's reality is your reality. Actually, it's always that way, but pretending customers think what you want them to think is much easier doing traditional marketing. You want to understand what customers think about your company, your products, your service, your attitude, the people they do have contact with, the people they don't have contact with, what they know they'd like from you, what they don't know they'd like from you, what pleases them. Then supplement customer input with the perspectives of those in your organization closest to customers.

- **Study your market.** Look outside at everything going around that touches your customers—the economy, your competition, government regulation, broad market trends that will help shape future customer behavior. And take an honest look at where you can fit into your customers' world.

- **Define your customers.** Based on what they tell you and how they behave, who are your customers? What are their "on" and "off" buttons? Do the interests of customer contacts and customer organizations coincide, or are they at odds?

- **Define yourself.** Put everything you can on the table—product information, your sales and distribution channels, your marketing, your packaging, your customer information management systems.

- **Identify your opportunities.** Make an informed, customer knowledge-based assessment of how you can create value for customers and yourself. Hey, you can start getting creative here—letting the imagination, which is now anchored in reality, take you to unexplored, un-thought of places.

- **Prioritize your opportunities.** You can't do it all. Not even with CRM. So you have to carefully select where to go first, and next.

- **Set your customer relationship strategies.** How are you going to get to where you decide to go? What will it take—from every corner of the company—for you to succeed?

That's how it flows, but where does it go? Best way to answer that is through some particularly interesting outcomes of this planning process—relationship-building opportunities identified that never would have surfaced in a traditional market planning process. And miracle of miracles, with luck and perseverance, most of these cases made it into the money-making phase—"CRM disease" and less-than-ideal technology notwithstanding.

The case of the long-lived capital equipment. A client that manufactured very expensive capital equipment wanted to get a higher return on a very expensive sales force. That was a thinly veiled threat to clamp down on sales and all their unnecessary "schmoozing" calls. Problem was, this equipment often lasted ten years or more—and even when clients owned numerous machines from my client, purchases were relatively infrequent and irregular. And if you hadn't been around enough when a customer decided to replace something, the competition could beat you in the door. So fewer calls could mean less business. Which meant that CRM, if used to *control* sales, could easily turn out counterproductive.

But stepping through the planning process and looking beyond surface sales or service stuff provided some useful insight. For one thing, most customers budgeted equipment replacement around hours of operation, which was relatively predictable. Furthermore, most machines had "hour-meters" attached to facilitate proper servicing. *Ergo,* if you stayed on top of hours of operation data, which the meters made possible—and you knew your customers replacement points—you could focus a substantial percentage of sales activity around specific replacement cycles.

Now, I don't mean to minimize the difficulty factors here. Acquiring replacement parameters and keeping up with hours of operation—plus factors like interest rates that could advance or retard a replacement decision—was hard work. Especially if we extended that to competitive equipment, which virtually all customers owned in addition to my client's stuff. So was building and maintaining product actuarial tables that would approximate replacement cycles for customers without predetermined parameters. But the potential increase in sales ROI was huge. And that wasn't the end of it.

By keeping all manner of information on the table in front of us, we also understood that manufacturing, which had to use batch runs rather than continuous production because of low production quantities, was guessing at the size of batch production runs. That meant losing sales opportunities to competitors by running out of stock—or having leftover stock that had to be sold at heavily discounted prices once new models came out, which happened almost annually because of intense product development efforts required to keep pace in an intensely competitive market. Not hard to figure out, if you had all the facts on the table, that accurate market demand projections were like gold.

Unfortunately, the most accurate demand forecasting method they'd found was looking at interest rates, holding up a wet finger to the breeze and winging it. And as it turned out, careful planning turned up an opportunity far greater than improving sales productivity—collecting sufficient field data on equipment age and hours of operation to support advanced, statistical calculations that could far more accurately forecast market demand in order to plan manufacturing run size.

Oh, and what was in it for my clients' customers? *Simplement.* They could get someone else to manage their maintenance schedules, which was a huge pain in the neck for customers.

Come to think of it, I had a high-tech case just recently with considerable overlay. Knowing the replacement cycle for hardware and software was a key to sales success. No meters on the outside to measure hours, though. Hell, stuff doesn't last that long. But another example of how using CRM to monitor customer (and even non-customer) inventory can give you a leg up on the competition.

Case of the mystery parts. Here's another situation where rooting around outside of narrowly-defined CRM input shed light on a big opportunity. Another manufacturing client was anxious to automate sales in order to better manage national accounts. Actually, even a cursory examination of business operations revealed that customers relied far more on customer service than sales—even for buying stuff—and that the critical information exchange missing was between sales and service. That made service the proper locus for CRM. But in working through our interview regimen with service staff— especially asking hard questions about customer attitudes—something else popped up.

My client's customers were really whizzed about incorrect parts shipments, which almost inevitably led to revenue loss. In fact, service got back, via Federal Express on my client's nickel, 15% of all parts shipped. Why? Seems that purchasing was buying manufacturing components on a "best price per lot" basis from lists of approved vendors. On some parts, such as electrical transformers, minor variances in mounting plates or hardware or lead wire colors or physical dimensions or whatever made one maker's parts incompatible with another's. And unfortunately, service had no idea whose parts were in which machines.

The base problem was that manufacturing wasn't keeping "string records" indicating which parts were in what units—and even if they had been, service had no access to manufacturing data.

No big deal to fix. All my client had to do was install some basic shop floor, record-keeping software and port the data to service. Classic front-office/back-office integration.

The case of the missing tape. Boy, is that ever a deceptive title. Rather than involving deep intrigue, this is a case of changing customers' perceptions by meeting them on their terms.

My client, known for its engineering prowess, designed and produced an extensive line of very high-tech tape products. They had already identified an opportunity to solve manufacturing problems in an entire consumer products industry dominated by four major players. Problem was, these potential customers wouldn't take tape seriously. "Tape is temporary." "Tape is what you use after you screw up." Attitudes like these. So they'd tried heavy trade journal advertising backed by direct selling. Nada. Not a dent. That's when we got the assignment.

We talked to customers. We talked to sales. We talked to marketing. We talked to everyone we could think of—asking rafts of questions, and listening. After doing lots and lots of listening, a clear picture started to emerge. The potential *buyers,* low- to mid-level engineers who were supposed to anticipate and solve manufacturing problems, had very little latitude to choose new products not already on their *approved* list. And purchasing was shortening the list, not expanding it. They didn't need new materials. But what they did need was help solving nasty materials specification issues thrown down to them, which they were seriously under qualified for solving. And they knew they were under qualified.

So here's our approach. We persuaded our client to offer free engineering support in the area where tapes could be used, rather than selling tape. Because these weren't current customers, we used direct marketing to offer these free services. But we also fished around in the industry and discovered that one of these four manufacturers was more lenient than others about accepting specs for "non-approved" materials. So we targeted the several thousand engineers in this company. Then we carefully screened all responses for information about free support—and offered to send engineers, not salespeople, to see the cream of the crop.

Try figuring this one out after spending two hours with sales, a few more hours with management, then designing a CRM software system.

The case of the dangerous decision. My client supplied retail hardware and home improvement chains with goods used by do-it-yourselfers (DIYs) but more so contractors who would pay more for longer lasting goods. One of the largest chains was limiting shelf space for my client's products. Their store planograms (shelf space allocations) were clearly skewed in favor of competitors. After failing to persuade their customer's corporate management to change this policy, they decided to bypass corporate and mount a database marketing program targeting individual store managers, who had at least some discretion of product placement. Emphasis on individual stores would vary based on size, openness of managers, their customer mix and other factors-information we could obtain from field sales, which serviced stores on a regional basis. Sounds like an ideal marketing automation opportunity, yes? No.

In fact, although it sounded great at first mention, it wasn't long before the whole idea was giving me the sweats. Like so much of database marketing, this was the antithesis of effective customer relationship management. For openers, this customer's corporate staff might have hung my client from a long yard-arm if they got one whiff of this end-run.

So we took our planning process and worked through it—assuming that our entire customer base was the half-dozen corporate managers making these adverse decisions. Rather than end-run them, we wanted to discover how we could provide more value to this customer in ways that would drive more favorable shelf placement for our client. And here's what we discovered.

Typical of all such situations, this customer was extracting as much co-op advertising money as possible from suppliers—and suppliers were trying to give as little as possible. In fact, these co-op negotiations often turn into donnybrooks with blood spilled and corporate egos bruised. That's just the biz. But in this case, my client's money was being used to advertise in media that missed my client's customers completely. This was lose-lose. But there was too much adversarial stuff going on to have a rational conversation about this. So here's what we devised.

Our planning had produced a clear profile of the most influential of these decision-makers. And what drove their decision-making most was good, old-fashioned loyalty to their company. They believed in getting their company the best shake they could, and they didn't believe that any supplier shared their concern. What came next was hardly rocket science. Do something good for their company—honestly and openly—and trust that they'll be willing to reciprocate.

Personally, I feared for my life when I suggested that our client take some of the end-run war chest and offer it to their customer as a voluntary *increase* in co-op contribution—along with using its considerable influence with non-competing but complementary suppliers to arrange some joint, new product introductions. But there was a *quid pro quo*. Part of the offer was a request that this customer would apply all co-op funds against the trade, where this money would do both client and customer the most good. Classic CRM. A unique case, in that neither work processes nor technology were part of the solution. But as I've been saying *(ad nauseum)*, CRM ain't software.

The case of the deadly poison. Boy, I really am taking some liberties with these titles. I have to be a tad less circumspect about this case to describe it. But that's okay, because regulatory changes have rendered the competitive aspects moot, and it has a few years on it. But I love telling it, because it's such a classic example of the good things that happen when you seek out sales, ask their opinions and listen to them.

Deal was that through stocking distributors, my client was selling the work-safety stuff workers wear while removing asbestos and other hazardous materials from buildings being reconstructed or demo'd. Think the estimate is we'll be done with the asbestos stuff about ten years from now. What a long haul. Anyway, their product was higher than average in price, offered distributors less than average margin and sold primarily on brand strength. But it wasn't selling enough. So my client asked us to figure out how to get on distributors' good sides so they would push my client's line.

Hey, sounds like a great situation for that new stuff called "partner relationship management" or "PRM." Excellent concept. Much more to do with CRM than marketing automation. But not this time.

Think about it. You're going to share information with distributors—including their customer information. They carry competing products and only sell yours when asked for specifically—and lose money when that happens. You want to market directly to their customers, which can only cost them money. Where's the win-win? Hey, that's what planning's for. Finding the win-win. And sometimes that takes changing the fundamental business proposition.

We had to fight some with our client before they let us take a couple of months to figure out what was going on and where the opportunities were. And the time was well spent. Two things happened during the planning process that completely changed the direction of this program. The first was about packaging. Packaging? In CRM? Yup. We noticed very detailed performance data on the outside of cellophane packaging surrounding this product. We asked if anyone one else had this data—and they didn't, because my client invested lots more in testing and QC than competitors did. Hey, might be important to some customers. So stick that in back of the ol' head for future use.

The second was interviews with sales people. My primary contact, who had a far better relationship with sales than most corporate managers, directed me to those having the greatest success with the line (which was far from all they sold). We interviewed around, discovered that contractors could give a whit about performance specs, which didn't help, and then hit pay dirt. Couple of guys in Texas had been working with a couple of architects helping them negotiate through impossible to understand EPA job safety requirements, which my client's sales force had to understand, so they would specify the right level protection. The right level was important because too high a level slowed the whole job down—and too low a level made the architect (or engineer) liable for any casualties. Oh, yeah? That perked up the ears. Better yet, these dudes had made up some funny tee-shirts about asbestos control and were wearing them into presentations with other architects, presentations they were being *asked* to do. Published specs, architects, liability, confusing regs, unsolicited requests for presentations. You get the picture. We just found the true customer—the one that has the most influence over which product gets purchased. What a customer-relationship building opportunity. Win-win to the nth degree.

Did we scramble. You never saw stuff come together so fast in your life.

Hey—that's all there is to it. It usually takes us two to four months of intense work with a client to complete this process, longer when we're creating an enterprise-wide customer focus where there isn't one. Regardless, trying to shortcut your way around planning is what takes the longest—sometimes forever, because you never get there. If you even know where *there is*. So don't cheat on the process. The only one you're cheating is yourself.

Redesigning Functional Activities

Before you go breaking down the conference room door with news of some magic elixir called "CRM" that's going to empower half the people in the company to get up close and personal with customers, consider these three facts.

1. CRM changes people's jobs.

2. Most people don't like that.

3. There's more of them than there are of you.

Add to it that the better designed your CRM implementation the *more* things have to change—and you'd better have plans in place to pull this off. Not to mention the active and visible support of perhaps even a higher muckety-muck than your team sponsor.

What's likely to change, activity wise, when you implement CRM? Let's start with sales.

- Sales will have to gather information, in addition to selling (which is why your CRM system had better offload lots of sales' admin time).

- Sales will become accountable for managing individual customer relationships, not just a territory.

- The daily life of sales people will wind up "on-screen" for all to see.

- More and more routine orders will come across the Internet, interfering with current compensation programs.

- Eventually, fewer sales people will have more responsibility—lots more.

- And, of course, every sales person will have to use a computer.

How much will all this change a day in the life of a sales rep? Unless your company is among the progressive minority, you're talking revolution, not evolution. Plus, lots of sales people are in sales so they don't have to mess with the very kinds of stuff CRM is going to make them do. Sure they'll adapt over time—some of them. But genetic imprinting ain't quick.

And once you're past the obvious changes, you get to deal with stuff like "loss of sociability" because sales transmits two-thirds of what they used to communicate by phone—and have to return to whatever office they work from a helluva lot less. Sound trivial? Think of it this way. Asking sales to stop and collect data is messing with their job. Asking them to reduce their human contact level with their co-workers is messing with their head.

Okay, now marketing.

- Traditional marketers, especially the ad guys, will find themselves working with more data and less media.

- Marketers will start supporting sales people, instead of spitting at them.

- Market analysts may do less quantitative number crunching and more qualitative issues analysis.

- Marketers will take data from sales rather than give data to sales.

- Marketing will have to grow bigger ears and lower its voice.

- Database marketers will finally have to *come clean* and acknowledge being old paradigm.

Hey, you talk about changes in job definition that change the type person you need on the job. You've got it. Big time. Marketing today is 99% inspiration and 1% perspiration. Marketing tomorrow, in CRM environments, is 1% inspiration and 99% perspiration. Or close to. Creative concepts don't mean squat in CRM. Branding means a lot less. And try asking a flowery talk copywriter who can spin a phrase at a drop of a hat to develop deflowered, non-promotional, informational copy suitable for downloading by today's no-nonsense customers.

And if you want an example of how hard marketing will fight back, just look at how they've already gunked up the Internet trying to use it as another TV channel. Useless banner ads everywhere. So much clutter that lots of us cruise the Net with our eyes closed. Hey, TV network, cable, the Net—peas in a pod. And look at how the database folks are shamelessly trying to take away every vestige of personal privacy by turning the Net into a spy service—so they can intrude on your business and your life like never before.

Next customer service.

- Customer service reps will likely report through marketing and sales—rather than to manufacturing or accounting.

- Service staff will have much more information at their fingertips, and much more responsibility as a result.

- Specific service people will often team with specific sales people to work with the same customers.

- And overall, service work will become more proactive and less reactive.

You catch a break here. Most service people will welcome changes like these. They're empowering—very empowering. But even here, you'll get some objections. And if you have field service folks, pay careful attention to sociability issues. Field service often suffers more on this score than sales.

Now, dare we say it, IT. Owie.

- IT has to cede some control. And not to just anyone, but to those "airheads" in sales and marketing.

- IT has to support sales, marketing and service—rather than telling them what to do.

- IT has to switch mindsets from using data to monitor and control operations to using data to satisfy customers. Talk about a rev-o-lu-tion…

- And above all, IT has to follow business strategy, not try to make it.

Okay, I am poking a little fun at IT because I grew up on the other side of the fence. While these changes are difficult to impossible for some IT folks and departments to swallow—many IT folks are doing a decent or better job, some a great job of making some pretty threatening changes. But some ain't all.

And hey, not too long ago I saw a client's top IT exec bolt over making customer service part of CRM and moving other legacy system functions out front as well. And getting IT to accept that all CRM technology runs on Windows operating systems and almost all on Microsoft's SQL Server databases and most utilizes Microsoft Exchange e-mail remains a constant challenge. So IT's transition is still a work in process—but it has started.

Think we're done yet, now that we've hit the "big four?" No way. CRM has much more impact than that. So let's continue with financial services—especially accounting.

- Billing may have to let sales and/or service trigger invoices—that flow from CRM software through the financial system to wherever—without passing accounting.

- Discretionary pricing may now rest solely with sales, with only "system checks" that require an approval outside of preset guidelines.

- Accounting staff will treat customers respectfully, mindful of the importance of customer relationships.

- Customer service will be set free to go where it belongs—to the front office with sales and marketing and on their CRM system.

Think about this. Nowhere in most companies are salespeople respected less than in accounting. Now, through CRM, we're going to empower sales with more financial decision-making authority? Whoa. Not an easy transition—often made harder by CRM's potential to cut into staffing needs in accounting. Hey, think about it this way. If every work activity is supposed to add value to customers—part of the credo of customer-centric companies—how does accounting fit that picture? Particularly in situations where accounting is taking already generated numbers and regenerating them on a different information system—or checking sales' work because sales "can't be trusted?" Doesn't quite pass the customer value sniff test.

From here, CRM-triggered activity changes become a lot more particular to particular companies, but here's what might happen.

- Product engineering accepts preliminary product configurations (partially machine-generated) from sales, rather than taking information from sales and starting from scratch.

- Engineering becomes part of the customer relationship team with greatly increased customer contact.

- Manufacturing lets sales prioritize run sequence according to the importance of individual customers waiting for orders.

- Delivery schedules become more important than manufacturing efficiency.

- Field-sales generated customer orders automatically trigger purchase orders, without purchasing intervention.

- Delivery schedules become more important than "lowest-cost" purchasing.

You get the picture. But how do you know which of these changes to functional activities will result from your CRM implementation? Simple. Well, relatively simple. Take the "data maps" tracking customer information flow that you developed to help get your team working on the same page—and if you didn't do them then, do them now—and *fix* them to reflect your customer relationship strategy. You can add lots of levity to this process by developing what I call "pictographs" to represent how customer information moves from function to function in your company. These pictographs use non-technical icons such as printers, stacks of paper, keyboards, black holes and other funny stuff that mark where stuff needs fixing. Cute. But what's especially cute is the outcome. These pictographs provide a superb base for redesigning functional activity around customers. And your redesign will tell you how things have to be organized from an org chart, reporting lines, re-division of labor standpoint. Here's a case where pictographs did, in fact, tell the story.

The case of the underutilized service technician. Now there's a proper title. And this one's very current, so I'm going to be extra circumspect.

We're working with a service company that has to send estimators/analyzers to customer sites first, then service crews. The drill is: customers call customer service; service sends estimators onsite to spec the work; estimators return to the office to research often extensive customer histories and even more extensive product resource files, then they meet with operations to estimate labor costs; estimators forward pricing to customer service; customer service calls the customer to try to close the job.

When we talked to their customers, our client got very high marks. Only complaints ran along the lines of, "Maybe a little expensive, but worth it." Talking to customers who split their business between our client and a competitor yielded little more than a desire to not rely on one vendor. But my client wasn't doing business with every desirable customer, even ones they targeted. And in today's marketplace, you can never, never, NEVER rest on your laurels. Sit very long and you get kicked where you sit.

So, using pictographs, we looked below the surface to look for service changes that would benefit customers that weren't occurring to customers—primarily, because they accepted certain parameters of this business as "the way things are done." And we found a couple of big changes with high impact potential—reducing total service cycle time, reducing the time and effort required of customers to set up service, and wringing more cost out of the process. Then we converted these changes into relationship improvement goals and worked with our client to develop appropriate strategies. Actually, we developed several—but the big one was to empower estimators to collapse the entire process into one onsite visit, which new CRM technology makes possible.

You don't need me to tell you how implementing this strategy will change estimators' jobs. Bottom line, they'll get a whole new set of activities and accountabilities. It's gonna be a different job. And everyone the estimators work with on the current work flow will experience activity changes as well.

You definitely don't need me to tell you that you don't show up at a staff meeting and announce changes like this as if they were new lunch times. But someone does need to tell a lot of CRM implementers who plow right ahead oblivious to what they're changing—or more accurately, what they're *attempting* to change.

Thankfully, our client's executive team has fostered a nonpolitical environment, which will greatly facilitate making changes like these. Unfortunately, not every outfit enjoys a low level of internal politicking, so it's on to the next chapter to deal with that issue. Before we pull out, you might want to trade your seat belt for a helmet.

Migration Management

Before we start, I gotta say this, "I am not an OD (as some of us call American Psychological Association Chapter XIV types trained in unsnarling corporate snarls—not to mention expert at keeping people from killing each other over who's got the bigger office)." Let me say it again,...No, you heard me the first time. But when you're implementing CRM, there are many times when you need an OD. And there are other times when you *really need one.* And that, by the way, is why I recommend having an HR exec on your CRM team. They're either trained in organizational development or (preferably) can bring in an outside specialist. You don't want to figure this out after the fact, after some crazed VP of something has emptied a whole quiver of arrows into your back.

> **Virtually every business with 50 or more people is populated with functional silos.**

Virtually every business with, say, 50 or more people is populated with functional silos. Now, farm language may seem out of place in an erudite work like this, but that's what they're called—*silos*. A silo is a functional department—you know, sales, marketing, service, IT, accounting, food service. More than that, it's a functional department that's assigned a certain set of functions by the organization. And over time (not much time, actually), silos start believing they own these functions just as you and I might own land, or "turf." Well, these silos turn into medieval fortresses with sword-wielding guards and spear-carrying horseman outside to protect the kingdom. And woe be to anyone who tries to steal a piece of the kingdom's turf—because turf is power and glory is number of soldiers and size of office.

So along comes CRM—disguised as a jackhammer—intent on blasting down some of these walls because CRM doesn't work when people from each silo work in isolation from the others. What we've got here is business designed around internal functions. And the customer is somewhere "out there." But when CRM arrives, these silos are supposed to up and circle 'round the customer and start dancing to the customer's tune. Did you ever see a silo dance?

And what are the chances, do you think, that's going to happen just because something called CRM showed up? Not great. And the bigger the organization, the less likely it's going to happen—unaided by very strong and unequivocal direction from the highest seat in the house. And even that's not enough in some cases.

That's why we're talking about migration management. It's an issue that's going to stick with us for a long time—like forever.

What's a poor CRM implementer to do about it? A couple of things. First, recognize that trouble's brewing before it brews. Sounds easy, eh? It's not. And let me pull another case out of my bag to demonstrate how yours truly managed to wander in front of a freight train.

The case of good being bad. Working on this project was among the high points of my career, when things were working. Which they weren't usually. But it had a happy ending, and I got to ride off into the sunset—*sans* horse, however.

This happened in my waning agency years, not long before I saw enough daylight for doing customer relationship stuff without masquerading as an "agency" (an *agency* that almost invariably found better ways than media advertising to connect with customers). We were hired by one of our 50 states to handle a sensitive assignment—using mass media to persuade older citizens that they should avail themselves of support services offered to help them "age in place" (at home) rather than wind up in assisted living. Seems that this particular state had the second highest percentage of older citizens in nursing homes in the country—and what with our aging population, that was going to get very expensive very fast. So we looked the situation over and set out to find out what our customers—older citizens and their adult children—wanted to do. And to make a long story short, we discovered that what our customers wanted most was for business to remember they were still part of the economy, not "dependents," and to create products and services designed for *them,* not for teenagers. Especially high on the priority list were what we later termed "chore" type services that frailing people have trouble with—simple home repairs, changing windows, getting groceries. And they wanted these services from absolutely trustworthy people who wouldn't take advantage of them.

That's how we came up with an entirely new concept we called, "Chore Corps." We lined up businesses willing to supply these products and services, often bundled together. Persuaded more they should do likewise. Provided training in working successfully with older consumers. Signed everyone to an ethics and standards pledge and told them we'd boot anybody out that violated 'em. Then we found a top-notch call center with sophisticated customer information management software of their own design that wanted to host this service and trained them, too. Next we set up a toll free phone number for older consumers to call to find the products and services they were looking for from businesses that had taken the pledge. Finally, we started using media to drive calls. Took a little to prime the pump. But before long we were forging and building relationships between our target customers and participating businesses—and between our call center resource and both. And doing a good deed, too. Or so we thought.

The "or so we thought" is the point of the story—and the CRM lesson. We barely got this sucker up and running because every state and federal agency around that had any dealings with *seniors* (their term, not ours) went after us with hatchets, pick axes, hand grenades, you name it. Now I'm far from an ultra-conservative, anti-government type—a lifelong Democrat, in fact—but the ensuing turf battle was disgusting. Didn't matter how much good we were doing. Seems like every silo in state government and social services felt we were encroaching on their "dependents" (how they saw the folks we called "customers"). Didn't matter if it was the Department of Health, Department of Human Services, Senior Federation, the nursing home associations, the Governor's office.

Didn't matter to them *what* we were doing—just that we'd set foot on their turf or some key constituent's (or contributor's) turf. Fortunately, in the end this deal got sold to the private sector—which had been our strategy since the beginning. But not before all of us involved had taken some heavy hits—and our sponsors from the state had been run out of state government. The good news is they were too sharp to stay there, and they all landed on their feet.

I still can't believe I'd been so naïve. Hey, I was speaking at the American Association on Aging national conference in the midst of this and had to admit "I forgot there was politics in government." Got a roar of laughter. Only thing funny about this deal for a long time. But it was a lesson well-learned.

Take heed. *Don't you forget there's politics in business.* Politics everywhere. Even where you'd least expect it. And be mindful that how much good CRM can do for the company may pale in importance to whether this department or that might have to give something up for the common cause—at least in the eyes of the silo manager affected. And that's why this stuff called "migration management" is so important.

You gotta see the opposition coming. Prepare for it. That's what migration management is about. Protect your project. Get your sponsor in front of you. Get your CEO to speak out—say, "This is where this company's going, closer to customers." And above all, get help diffusing this stuff before it starts. That's the mistake we made with Chore Corps. We let the battle lines get set up, then we tried to duck. Instead, we should have assessed who might oppose us because of an imagined (or real) threat to their turf, then invited them into process, negotiated with them, brought in a muckety-muck to make clear that this was the State's direction (a benefactor we didn't have, because we'd lulled ourselves into thinking the State would back anything this good for both citizens and state).

And migration management doesn't just happen on the management level. Remember all the activity changes we discussed last chapter? Every change is a migration that you need to think about and, if necessary, manage so it happens and happens the right way.

Some of this stuff you can figure out and deal with directly using your intuitive skills and common sense. But other times you'll need someone skilled in helping people and companies through transitions. And that's yet another reason for having a strong team sponsor. Bringing in an OD is a senior-level decision. Getting one onboard is almost always a sponsor- or even higher-level job. And that's as far as I'm going to take this because I don't like stepping outside my training and experience. But see the last chapter, "Help!" for some additional resources.

Now, add migration management to your preceding activity planning to your preceding customer relationship planning— and you've got your CRM strategy. Not only that, but the hardest work is behind you, which is good, because by now you've really worked up a sweat. But best of all, the chances that you'll survive CRM have shot way, way up.

From here on, everything flows from your strategy. Process re-engineering, software selection and design, even training— like water over a dam. Okay, not quite. But you're going downhill from here on (and I mean that in the positive sense).

IV. CRM Nuts & Bolts

Perspective Check

Now for the shocker. Before you started reading, there's a good percentage chance you thought this book would be 95% software and process talk, 5% other stuff. Or 90%-10% or even 80%-20%. Well, maybe you didn't. If not, kudos. Regardless. Point is, if you do your due diligence up front, in the planning stage, the rest of CRM is *relatively* easy. You've already made the tough calls. You've already determined your direction. You've already written your project script. Now all you have to do is follow it.

But if you're determined to avoid all that time-consuming, boring, dirty work up front—go ahead. It's a fool's errand because you're going to spend your entire deployment trying to go back and do what needed doing before diving into the likes of process re-engineering and software selection and software build-out. And you're never going to get any of it done right. Just remember when you point the finger after you fail— you've got your other three fingers pointing back at, guess who? Gosh, I guess I could be a little nicer than that, but who listens to *nice?*

You can imagine why I cringe when I hear consultants and software companies tell CRM implementers they can start CRM with process re-engineering. Not *real* CRM that leads to customer-centricity, you can't. No way. Internally-focused SFA and simple service automation? Sometimes. But those pitching you upper-case CRM as process-driven, not strategically driven, are pied pipers. And when they get you to the edge of the cliff, they step aside and let you walk over. And if you're still breathing after falling on hard rock from 150 feet, you might hear a few rounds of "Company culture was wrong," or "They just didn't execute." No Charlie, you did the executing.

> **Those pitching you upper-case CRM as process-driven, not strategically driven, are pied pipers.**

Hear it the right way from Steve Dorio, president of IMT Strategies.

> Most companies will need to put far better business plans in place to manage the complexities of assembling and integrating CRM programs across their organizations. Those that don't will fail to achieve business impact.[15]

Nice impact, though, when you crash land.

Now, see why "Nuts & Bolts" stuff like process re-engineering and software represents only a small segment of this book? CRM survival doesn't happen here. Your fate is pretty much preordained. Okay, you can mess up here bad enough to undercut an effective strategy. But you really have to work at it—as in letting a persuasive software dude talk you out of your CRM strategy because his system doesn't work that way.

---

[15] As quoted in "Death of the Call Center," Daniel Costello, *Sales & Marketing Automation*, January 2000.

But hey, even the kind of reversible reverses you might suffer back here leave their bumps and bruises and often significant extra expense. So there's stuff we should talk about so you not only survive, but come through in good health. We'll hit the high points here—especially your approach to process re-engineering and your software selection method. And for those readers who want a very detailed road map through deployment, we're about to develop a "Customer Relationship Management Deployment Guide" that butts up with the existing *Customer Relationship Management Planning Guide*. Should be available on our site and on the Amazon site in June or July 2000. Good for following, but it's going to make terrible reading.

Re-Engineering Work Processes

There are two principal ways that CRM implementers who get in trouble with process re-engineering get into trouble. Oh, there's lots of other stuff you can do, but these two are the ones that can really set you back—and sometimes force you to retrace your steps.

The first—and I know this is going to sound like it's out of left field—is letting software drive your work processes rather than your work processes driving the

> **NEVER, NEVER, NEVER let CRM software dictate how you do stuff.**

software. "Software-aided re-engineering" they call it. Surprised I'd take that position, eh? Well, let me go on record saying, NEVER, NEVER, NEVER let CRM software dictate how you do stuff. Obviously, every software system does this in minor ways, but you can't let this happen on the big stuff.

Here's a little history on this topic. The last great wave of technology preceding CRM was Enterprise Resource Planning (ERP). ERP was supposed to do for the back office what CRM is supposed to do for the front office—connect and coordinate everything going on. As it turned out, most ERP implementations were painful. Some were very painful. Some never took. And in a surprisingly large percentage of cases, customers can't glue their back-office operations back together after ERP dismantled whatever systems, automated or manual, were already in place—and then replaced them with stuff so inappropriate or intricate that customers couldn't run on it.

I've had several clients that were permanently injured by bad ERP implementations. And customers are starting to fight back. Some high-profile, abused companies have started suing software companies for what they perceive as dishonestly downplaying the difficulty factor in deploying their systems. Could be as big as asbestos for the liability lawyers, given the number of ERP implementations gone sour.

What went wrong with so many ERP deals? Process re-engineering, that's what. The whole theory behind ERP is that whatever software system you buy includes "best practice" processes the customer is supposed to adopt. But "best practices" for whom? On the theory that all manufacturing companies run more or less alike—and samo, samo for distribution, food processing, you name it—ERP tries to solve everyone's problems relatively the same way. Force fit, in other words. Of course, you can modify ERP systems to a point to fit your individual needs, but you're still dealing with a relatively inflexible system infrastructure that breaks, not bends, if you torque it a whole lot.

And there's another common problem with ERP. It usually bases underlying process management assumptions on predictable conditions. Like all materials will be delivered when we think they will, machinery won't break down, the flu won't disable a quarter of the work force for a week, and even—get this—that customer order flow is predictable. The attitude

behind ERP is that we're gonna use machines to run machines—
and we'll expect employees and customers to act like machines.
Never mind the horrible misassumption about customer behavior, back-office operations themselves often fail to achieve
sufficient predictability for these assumptions to hold.

Now, in fairness to the ERP folks, ERP technology has to
handle lots more rote tasks than CRM stuff. So many tasks that
maintaining ERP software would be difficult without considerable internal, unbendable system structure. Still, imposing an
ERP system's structure on an organization that can't comfort-
ably operate under the resulting work rules usually means
spending gobs of money to trade one set of problems for
another. And unfortunately, this *force fit* syndrome has carried
over into the CRM world.

Stark evidence of the rigidity of most ERP systems is their
inability to support a new approach to process management
originally called "Theory of Constraints," now called "constraints management" because it's no longer a theory, and
commonly referred to by those who practice it as "TOC." The
problems most ERP systems have supporting TOC emanate
from TOC's basis in conditions of *un*predictability. TOC
assumes stuff doesn't happen the way it's supposed to lots of the
time—and deals with that (we'll explain how in just a minute).
Get the feeling that ERP and TOC are like oil and water?

Now, what do you think happens when an ERP software
systems developer decides to offer CRM as an *adjunct* to ERP
(ERP guys often refer to CRM in such diminutive terms)? The
mindset that produces process rules that are often too rigid for
the back office will almost inevitably produce stuff that's a vir-
tual straight jacket for the front office. That's why I believe most
ERP-extension CRM software is dead on arrival.

If you remember one thing out of this chapter, remember
these three related points.

- ERP systems, rightly or wrongly, are designed for machine processes supported by humans.

- CRM systems are, or should be, designed for human processes supported by machines.

- The external factor most important to ERP is vendor supply, over which companies have at least some measure of control. The external factor most important to CRM is customers, over which we have damn little control.

Unfortunately, lots of CRM systems, even those developed by CRM folks, are designed for machine-like processes run by humans—and assume that we can somehow control customers. That's why you'll hear CRM salespeople say, "Our system adapts to your business," out of one side of their mouths and, "Here's how you work using our system," out of the other side. Not surprisingly, it's the adaptable-to-your-business side that speaks before the sale, and the here's-how-you-work side that speaks after. And that's why I'm so adamant about giving CRM software vendors *your* operating requirements and saying, "It's our way or the highway." But I'm stealing thunder from the next chapter, which deals directly with software.

But on to best practices for process re-engineering in a CRM environment.

Once you've developed your CRM strategy and determined which functional activities must change as a result, the next step is re-engineering work processes to fulfill your new or redesigned functions. And don't stop there. While you're at it, take this opportunity to clean up lots of processes that don't have to change but could be improved—improved often by breaking down silo walls to free up departmental islands of information; or by using CRM technology to automate manual tasks, especially customer information hand-offs from front office to back office but even pure back-office stuff; or by removing system impediments to free and easy flow of customer information throughout the enterprise.

How do you go about doing all this? Easy. Take your pictographs, the revised ones, and break each one down into detailed work processes. Hey wait a minute, though. We're talking about information flow. Aren't we supposed to be talking about work flow? Yup. But I'll let you in on another little secret. CRM-related work flow rides just above customer information flow, step-by-step, task-by-task. Map customer information flow first, then it's really easy to overlay CRM work processes. Much

> **CRM systems should be designed for human processes supported by machines, not machine processes supported by humans.**

easier than starting at the process level, if that makes any sense.

When you do map out your workflow, you may find that you don't enjoy it very much. But hang in there (which is different than "hang yourself"). We do this stuff with process mapping automation software. Check out the output on the next page. Pretty slick, no? Too bad this dandy software arrived too late to save my remaining hairs.

So now you've got all this process stuff laid out in front of you. The next natural step is to identify resources required, especially human resources, because we're dealing mostly with front-office work, and not so directly with production machinery or materials inventory or other tangibles. And what appears to be the logical way to approach resource allocation is figuring out how much work has to be done at each step—and how many people with how much and what technology support will be required to do it. Makes sense, doesn't it?

RFQ Process

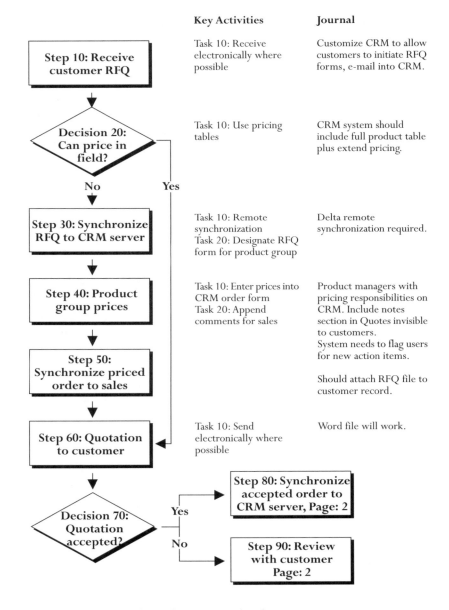

Key Activities   **Journal**

Step 10: Receive customer RFQ
Task 10: Receive electronically where possible
Customize CRM to allow customers to initiate RFQ forms, e-mail into CRM.

Decision 20: Can price in field?
Task 10: Use pricing tables
CRM system should include full product table plus extend pricing.

No   Yes

Step 30: Synchronize RFQ to CRM server
Task 10: Remote synchronization
Task 20: Designate RFQ form for product group
Delta remote synchronization required.

Step 40: Product group prices
Task 10: Enter prices into CRM order form
Task 20: Append comments for sales
Product managers with pricing responsibilities on CRM. Include notes section in Quotes invisible to customers.
System needs to flag users for new action items.

Step 50: Synchronize priced order to sales
Should attach RFQ file to customer record.

Step 60: Quotation to customer
Task 10: Send electronically where possible
Word file will work.

Decision 70: Quotation accepted?
Yes
No

Step 80: Synchronize accepted order to CRM server, Page: 2

Step 90: Review with customer Page: 2

*Note how the CRM technology requirements
are listed in the right hand column*

Whoops. We just fell into the "balanced flow" trap. Imbedded in this "sufficient resources at every station" logic is the assumption that you'll have predictable, balanced workflow. It's the same assumption ERP folks make that gets them in so much trouble—and CRM workflow is far less predictable.

TOC gets you out of this trap. Instead of assuming high predictability, TOC helps you cope with more random events. Instead of trying to minimize resources to just what you need to get the job done, if everything goes right, TOC focuses on maximizing

> **Instead of assuming high predictability, TOC helps you cope with more random events.**

throughput under a variety of conditions—including activity spikes that lead to severe *bottlenecks* under balanced flow systems. Your assignment, if you accept the TOC way, will be to:

- Identify critical *constraints*—the points in your marketing, sales, service process chain where work flow is most likely to become constricted, given an increased volume of work.

- Re-engineer processes and redistribute resources to move your primary constraint to the most difficult, most expensive place to add capacity.

- Maximize throughput affordably by maximizing work potential at the primary constraint (and often at second or third process points) that can constrict flow.

In a CRM environment, field sales is among the more likely primary constraints. So is in-person customer service. Other candidates include product engineering for made-to-order (MTO) products, inquiry qualification before sales leads go to field sales, and call center order processing in environments where marketing produces bursts of orders.

Classic examples of work-flow bottlenecks include lack of field sales time to build customer relationships and/or follow up on new customer inquiries; long and sometimes interminable hold times for customer service calls (a phenomenon that has already wounded many consumer e-commerce players), bins full of unprocessed sales inquiries, including e-inquiries; orders/inquiries lost because of long wait times for call pick up. Solutions for these bottlenecks include removing every possible administrative responsibility from sales, and automating the rest; rerouting routine information requests through websites; outsourcing inquiry qualification and fulfillment; and rerouting commodity purchases and informational inquiries through the web.

Hey, this stuff is simple, right? I'd be tempted to say, "yes," were it not for the insensitivity to both sales/service staff and customers shown by so many companies dealing with these issues. For example, using CRM to try to beat more productivity out of sales, rather than free up their time so they can spend more time with customers. Reminds me of the CEO who asked if GPS could be installed in laptops so they could spot sales people parking their cars (and their laptops) at the golf course. If you're not familiar with GPS, it's that global positioning stuff fishermen use to return to their favorite spot in the middle of the lake. Great marriage of IBM and Bass Pro.

And of course, let's not forget the web-hos who relegate *all* customer service to the web, totally whizzing off customers. Or the all business types that want to use CRM to monitor service rep productivity in "call turn" terms, rather than "issues resolved." Don't you love the software service reps stuck watching their watches (or the time ticker on their screen, actually) while they try to resolve a glitch they don't understand? "Sounds like a hardware problem to me." Not to mention the genii that asked customers to self-qualify for decent treatment by filling out a long, intrusive form before they're allowed to request information, with nothing offered to the customer in return. And last but not least, the web, webbies marketing over the Internet to customers that don't want to buy electronically. Hey if they're not with it they're not worth it. Right?

Yeah, TOC can be easy—at least top-level TOC can be (we'll get further into TOC applications in *The Customer Relationship Management Deployment Guide* that's on the way). But you gotta use your head when you use it. But that's true of about anything, *n'est pas?*

Oh, and as always, one more thing. At the risk of repeating myself, remember that CRM process management in most companies is still about people dealing with people with some machine support—not machines processing raw materials with as little human intervention as possible. So don't take process re-engineering much past the "sequence of events" level. Even that will run up 30 to 50 pages of flow charts in most companies, if you roll in back-office functions related to specific customers. But not a big deal, thanks to flow-charting automation software. You may hear the "drill down deep" line from some big name consulting firms that are just dying to descend upon you with armies of MBAs—ready and willing to map sales processes in particular right down to which hand holds the bologna sandwich and which wipes off the ketchup moustache. All at an extraordinary hourly rate. Hey, I'm an MBA too, and it means about zilch in my practice—especially compared to street-level sales and sales management experience. Don't fall for this hokus-pokus.

Hopefully, that was clear enough to give you the big picture on process stuff. The next step further into process re-engineering and TOC is a giant one, so we'll call it a chapter here, before I offend anyone else. But just you think TOC, and you'll be a lot further along to start with then you will after the *descent of the MBAs.*

Supporting With Software

Sadly, if you ask a hundred companies that haven't yet tried on CRM or learned much about it, "What's the most important CRM decision you're going to make?" better than half will say, "Selecting the right software." That's why so many misguided CRM projects start with software selection. If I was the caustic type I'd say most of them end there, too. But I'm a nicer guy than that, eh?

Funny thing is, after I've completed planning a CRM project through the process level, the software is damn near chosen. Typically, the job requirements have whittled the seemingly endless list of software options down to five, maybe only three, or even one system that's clearly superior for the task at hand. But I keep up with the CRM software market much better than team members who are doing this for the first time. So let's talk selection to help you find your best choices.

Like it or not, folks deploying ERP have to use "screen in" software selection criteria. That is, they have to find positive matches, or as close as then can come, to what they need to run their business. ERP software is typically too inflexible to do otherwise. Of course the big losers in this bunch let software dictate how they're going to do things, but we're assuming better judgment than that. But CRM software selectors can do otherwise—meaning they can use "screen in" selection criteria to identify which CRM software systems support their *modus operandi*.

There's a world of difference between the two approaches. While ERP selectors have to immerse themselves in what each system can and can't do, CRM selectors can circulate their requirements and make software sellers come to them. And that's precisely what you should do.

Now that you've developed your CRM strategy, determined functional activities *and* designed new or re-engineered work flow, you're ready to determine what type of technology support you need.

> **CRM software selectors should use "screen in" selection criteria to identify which CRM software systems support their *modus operandi*.**

A great way to start is to take a complete set of new process maps (meaning draw them up, if you haven't already) and identify required CRM functionality for each process step and task you've defined. And don't forget to include what data you need to access—and what "wizards" you need in order to reduce complex steps like preparing a proposal or pricing an order or researching product detail down to mouse clicks. When you finish, you're already 80% of the way to developing your CRM technology specs.

Next, you need to identify additional functional characteristics for your CRM system. This takes a bit more exposure to CRM software than step one, but here's a basic checklist of requirements to consider.

Primary functionality. Despite claims to the contrary, few if any CRM software systems perform equally well for sales, service and marketing management. Most started in one of these three primary areas and migrated into the others in order to become "full service CRM."

Many of these *migrations* were actually acquisitions—for example, a sales automation company buying a service automation company. However, the majority of the acquisition-driven integrations of disparate functions disintegrate in use.

Another type of migration is a sales automation company attempting to build a service component. Problem here is that customer service software is far more complex than sales automation software, and the majority of these attempts underestimated the difficulty factor and floundered.

A third variety of migration is from marketing automation to sales and service automation. Marketing automation is so dissimilar to the other two that they might as well have tried going from logistics to sales automation. Going from sales/service to marketing automation makes far more sense because sales and service feed data into marketing, while there's relatively little connectivity the other way. I don't know of a single one of these attempts that's succeeded.

Overall, the best migrations have been from a customer service base into sales. But there aren't many of them.

As a rule of thumb, start with your primary need, sales or service, and match that to the software system's foundation. Then, make sure that the other side can handle your needs. "Marketing's our primary need," you say? Then you're probably not doing CRM, but database marketing instead—in which case you need to go read another book. And regarding marketing automation—don't be afraid to go "best of breed" by combining your favorite marketing package with the sales/service package you select. That's because integration between sales/service on one side and marketing on the other is about exchanging data rather than integrating functions or work processes. As long as both sides are running on SQL Server databases (or open architecture anything), you should be fine going best of breed. And if the marketing side is storing data in some complex data warehouse, just make sure the data dump can receive data from sales and service and send a little back.

Open architecture. You may be integrating data out on laptops with CRM server data with office productivity software to ERP data and who knows where else. You're safest bet is to stay with CRM software that observes tight Microsoft standards—even if your back-office folks are running Oracle databases or heavy on UNIX or Linux at the points of integration with CRM. Your IT folks should help you keep this straight. But if you hear mention of running CRM on other than a Microsoft SQL Server database—run, don't walk, for a second opinion. Hey, a little exercise never hurt anyway.

Two more things you don't want to hear about: using CRM software that doesn't utilize a fully relational database at the laptop level and modifying "groupware" such as Lotus Notes® in place of using CRM software. These *faux pas* typically occur in small business environments, but it never ceases to amaze me how many larger companies stick their feet in one of these buckets.

Off-line functionality. That's a fancy way of saying, "Do your sales people or other remote users need full data and full functionality when they're *not* dialed into your CRM server or connected over the Internet?" Problem is that lots of e-whiz CRM software systems are totally web-based, and sales people have to access not only most of their data but most of their software via Internet or telephone connection to the web database and web server. That's what the "thin client" systems so many CRM software vendors are over-hyping do for you. What an expression of disdain for field sales people! If you have field sales people employed by your company, a good rule of thumb is to rule out any software that does not offer reps 100% data and 100% functionality while they're untethered (which is a fancy way of saying disconnected from the server). Hey, you might settle for 98%, but not a percent less—okay?

Integration capabilities. Remember that CRM includes data integration with back-office systems. A well-designed system provides facilities for exchanging data with common data-bases—although not necessarily your behemoth main frame, which you can't get in and out of with anything short of dyna-mite. And don't get fooled by, "We've got a strategic relationship with…(this ERP vendor or that)." Most of these *relationships* are all show and no go.

User modification. Static businesses don't survive today—at least not most of them. So don't pick software assuming that your business is going to need the same CRM software support tomorrow as today. Hey, any software can be modified after the fact. The question is, can *you* do it, or can you contract an out-side resource to do it for less than a gazillion dollars an hour and a six-month wait? Tomorrow's CRM software systems are going to be giant toolboxes that let you create what you need—at least the good ones are gonna look like that. But we're not there yet. So pick a package that either you can modify—or more than a select few software development contractors can modify.

That's a broad list of what to consider about the software products themselves. But you'd better go a step further and look at the companies that sell these things. Here's what you should sniff out through some thorough questioning, with assis-tance perhaps from an experienced financial type and definitely from a few folks from IT.

Financial stability. The number of CRM software suppliers has dropped from 300 to 400 several years ago to about 100 today. Mergers and acquisitions account for some of that, but financial instability has been the big stick knocking them out.

Be especially careful checking out start-ups or companies with declining market share or less-than-stellar financial results.

Target customers. Many CRM software providers claim they serve the middle market, but most of that is bovine waste matter. Only a few major CRM software sellers provide effective customer support to customers with less than 100 users after the sale—and in some cases to customers with less than 1,000 users. On the flip side, some sellers of mid-sized systems claim they can wire the world, or darn close. In either case, ask for references of jobs with companies similar in size to you.

Reseller network. In 1997 when I wrote the predecessor to this book, *The Sales Automation Survival Guide,* I cautioned against doing business with VARs (value-added resellers that supposedly can tailor a system to your specific needs). Back then, most VARs ranged in skill from deficient to incompetent. Today, that's changed—at least for some VAR networks it has. Why the difference? Primarily the increased presence of software systems integrators and back-office system resellers in CRM. Hey, ERP sales are falling. Gotta go where the bucks are. The good news about these folks is that they understand technology, which the first wave of SFA resellers did not. The bad news is that some barely understand the concept of CRM—or even the workings of the front office. But that's still an improvement, because the SFA guys were mostly out peddling software with scant understanding of how to apply it anyway. Something gained and nothing lost.

> **If you get lots of shuckin' and jivin' instead of straight answers, hit the rip cord.**

Another little hint here—if your IT department is either weak or overwhelmed or both, the presence of a strong VAR to help with data integration may outweigh the advantages of one

CRM software system over another. The right CRM system with the wrong integration can make a good project go bad.

Hey, you gotta case this stuff out carefully. And if you get lots of shuckin' and jivin' instead of straight answers, hit the rip cord. Or better yet, since you're in charge, open that trap door underneath whoever's serenading you.

Okay, now you're ready to rock 'n roll. You've got your process maps and CRM functionality. You've written up your requirements. And you're ready to screen out systems and companies that don't pass muster. But which companies and systems do you screen? Yeah, I can hear your heavy breathing. You want *names*. You want me to tell you what to buy. We'll, I'M NOT GONNA DO IT. Not for three reasons.

First, the software sands are shifting rapidly. Whatever's on top today may be sliding down the pole tomorrow—or at least next year. Second, I don't know whether you're going to go through a reseller and who that might be. Third, I don't know what you need, you do!

But I'm not going to leave you high and dry, either.

If you're not up to speed on the CRM software market, here are three ways to go about making an intelligent selection.

Way #1.

- **Work with a software neutral consultant who has no financial interest in whatever you select.** That's my favorite way, because I'm one of these folks.

Way #2.

- **Call Rich Bohn of the Denali Group.** Rich runs a software selection practice that helps clients, who have done their due diligence, select appropriate software. He knows more about the CRM software market than any six or eight people I know. You can find his particulars in the last chapter, "Help!"

- **Then, attend one of DCI's more or less quarterly CRM conferences.** The exposition floor is littered with CRM software sellers for you to meet and look over with a jaundiced eye. A word of warning, however, wear your gas mask when you hit the exhibit floor. The exhaust fumes from some booths can overcome you.

Way #3.

- **Go to DCI first.**

- **Then, call Bohn.**

What's next? Contact a short list of software sellers (typically five to seven) and tell them precisely what you're looking for—and ask them to respond with their specific capabilities, in detail. And you may want to ask for the name of their best reseller in your environs. Just tell them that the final decision may rest on reseller technology expertise. You'll get referred to their best.

Then, pare your list down to ideally not more than three. But be nice to those you don't select. You'll never know when you're going to need friends—or a new job, if you're project goes south.

Finally comes the fun part. Show and tell. Ask for demonstrations that show all the functionality you've specified—and ask each company what more they can do for you. Supply everyone with a synopsis of your business including number of CRM users and their roles. If they don't read it carefully before presenting, throw them out. Unceremoniously. If they tell you that you should arrange work flow their way rather than your way, throw 'em out. Even less ceremoniously. If they listen to you and grasp what you need—and honestly tell you what they can do for you, and can't—take them seriously and work with them to find middle ground between what you want and what they can't quite deliver.

> **Ask for demonstrations that show all the software functionality you've specified.**

This is a give and take deal. But remember, you're in the driver's seat. Oh yeah, and the inevitable "one more thing." Let your IT folks give them a good once over (or maybe a twice over) to sniff out hot air and sales spew masquerading as substance—especially with regard to systems integration issues.

Once you select, it's build-out time. Time for the seller to make the software do what the seller said it would do. And keep this in mind. As CRM gets more complex, the day when we need to get detailed, written performance commitments laying out system functionality is upon us. You don't ever want to go into CRM thinking about hanging a CRM seller by the agreement they signed. But stuff happens. And the more complex the systems, the more it happens. And hey, written agreements also protect technology vendors from project creep, which also happens—a lot.

And now, only one more little subject to cover, visa CRM software.

We still have to address an option to *buying* software. *Renting* it from an application service provider (ASP) that sticks software on their web server for you to access via browser. Might even modify the software some for you. ASPs in CRM are generating lots of buzz right now. Supposed to be the wave of the future.

Want my opinion of ASPs in CRM? No? Well, I'll share yet another opinion from the IT camp where they're supposed to love this stuff.

> The Web application servers reviewed in this week's issue are evidence of the momentum behind browser-based application access. And they're the culmination of a technology whose time will soon pass.[16]

This dude gets even rougher on ASPs, but there's lots of tech talk in the really gritty passages. And, you might wonder, is this a safe way to go? I'll spare you my opinion again.

> When and if the Internet becomes a reliable network, companies renting these applications will need service-level guarantees that have stiff financial penalties for loss of service.[17]

Doesn't sound like you ought to trust 'em. Besides, your field staff has to be connected to the Internet to use this stuff. Bad, bad, bad.

Enough, already. With 90% of the words spoken about CRM being about software, I don't want to add to the imbalance.

---

[16] "The End of the Web as We Know It," Sean Gallagher, *Information Week,* April 5, 1999.

[17] "Rental Office is Uninhabitable," Michael Caton, *PC Week,* November 16, 1999.

Training & Launch

This is my last "one more thing." I promise. But I'm not ready to quit quite yet.

If you've done your spadework so far, there's no way you're going to short shrift training. The need to prepare folks for their new roles, work processes and technologies will be staring you in the face. As will the necessity, for most of you, to launch CRM in stages. That's especially true of adopting CRM technology. You can't throw too much technology at non-technologists and expect them to be immediately facile at running it. And if you get people way in over their heads, you may have to let them all the way out of the water to recoup before sending them back in again.

In fact, even if you take things gradually you can get into a heap of trouble over something that happened (or should have happened) way back when you were developing your CRM strategy. That *something* is your *training budget*—which, by the way, often should be larger than your technology budget, particularly in larger companies.

Amidst all the expense of implementing CRM, it's easy to start cutting corners in order to have more money for—you guessed it—usually software.

Don't. Especially if the money you're cutting is training money. Too many CRM implementations come down to launch-time without enough dough for training. Get the money upfront, and adopt a hands-off policy. This isn't social security money that gets tapped into whenever there's a shortfall somewhere else. Lock it up.

> **Amidst all the expense of implementing CRM, it's easy to start cutting corners in order to have more money for software.**

And that ought to lock up your CRM implementation. We've certainly not covered all the details. That's what "Planning Guide" and the soon to be "Deployment Guide" are for. But I hope we've filled the potholes, cleared the fallen trees and killed off the bad guys that are most likely to impede you on your way to CRM success.

Good luck.

V. Sidebars

Just as when I finished *The Sales Automation Survival Guide,* I've managed to leave out several important topics—and managed not giving several important topics sufficient emphasis. So here's a little make-up work. And bye the bye, these little sidebars are important stuff you may want to copy and pass around. Don't sweat the copyright stuff (but only on the following pages, please!).

Silence From Above

In most CRM implementations, the most important player is the CEO. That's not a mantle most chief executives want to accept. "Not strategic enough to warrant my time." "That's a middle management job." "My managers need to work things out themselves, that's what we pay them for." Wrong. Wrong. Wrong.

1. **CRM is the first step in the process of reorienting a business around its customers.** If it fails, and the majority do fail, so does the effort to become a customer-focused business. It doesn't get much more strategically focused than that.

2. **Putting middle management in sole charge of CRM increases the chances of failure to almost 100%.** To pass on a saying of an organizational development buddy, Ralph Jacobson, "Change the information flow, change the company." CRM changes information flow dramatically, and it changes the company dramatically. Middle managers aren't empowered to change companies.

3. **CRM breaks down management silos.** Asking even senior executives to give up departmental or divisional authority, even subordinate themselves to other executives, is serious stuff. Smart CEOs don't expect their senior managers to just roll over and "take one for the Gipper." The smart ones know they need to *proactively* design a new, customer-centered organization—and take the lead in implementing their new organization.

Part and parcel of a CEO (or comparable senior executive) washing their hands of CRM is the train wreck that occurs at the middle management level—with the poor middle manager who gets run over while trying to implement CRM. Every consultant I know in the business has seen this happen, often multiple times. It makes us sick to our stomachs. And it leaves us wanting to throttle those who let it happen.

Here's what goes down. A middle manager gets assigned to design and implement CRM, from strategy to technology. If they're lucky, they have a reasonably strong sponsor. They stroke, soothe, cajole, jawbone, finesse their way through all the normal hurdles that CRM implementers face. Miraculously, they make it through strategy to deployment—to the nuts and bolts phase. But they're about to do something too visible and too significant for a middle manager to get credit for in their corporate environment.

So with the blessing of the CEO or whomever, in sashays some corporate climber with visions of career advancement dancing in their head. They proceed to take over the project in a very paternalistic way. "Nice job so far, but I'd better finish this for you." Boy, do they ever finish it.

First, the whole focus of the system starts changing from benefiting the customer and relationship managers to benefiting corporate management. Next, you start hearing talk like, "they'll use the system (CRM technology) because we tell them to use it." Then our corporate climber perverts CRM into a flashy Internet side show that feeds nothing but egos. Meanwhile, some poor middle manager gets chewed up and spit out onto the corporate dung heap.

You can blame the interloper—and they surely deserve all the blame you can heap on them. But they could only trash the project because somebody let them. The CEO. The sponsor. A bunch of folks who were supposed to be looking out for the company.

If you want a second opinion about this, silent CEOs, read "An Open Letter to the CEO" that concludes Peppers and Rogers' *Enterprise One To One.*[18] The tone may be more palatable than mine. But the message is the same. We've all been there. Seen that. Enough of that. We feel for the innocent and loyal employees who get used. And we recognize the damage that your silence and complicity do to the whole enterprise. So should you.

You cannot afford to be silent.

---

[18] Opus cited.

Ageism

I treat my clients with great respect, or at least try to. After all, they're my customers. They're paying me. And while they deserve my honest and objective thinking, they deserve that delivered in a reasoned and professional manner.

But when I hear someone say, "it's a good opportunity to lose some of our older folks," or "the old guys will never learn to run computers," or similar stuff, I get my dander up. Deploying CRM technology is no excuse for discriminatory employment practices, intentional or otherwise.

The conscious stuff is actually easy to deal with. I won't work with a client who intentionally practices ageism. I can't change a discriminatory mindset, and I won't stick around to try.

But the unconscious stuff is another matter. CRM generates a very substantial amount of unintentional ageism. Here's how it happens.

You just know that so-and-so is totally averse to using a computer, any kind of computer, for any purpose. You have a legitimate need to require your relationship managers to work, on computer, with your CRM system. You know so-and-so won't do it, so you figure you'll have to lose them.

But wait a minute. *Why* won't this person use a computer? Why will they hold out, at the risk of losing their job?

Usually because they're intimidated. They lack confidence they can learn to use one. They feel inferior to younger employees who can't yet carry their briefcase in terms of forging and maintaining customer relationships—but who are very facile "on the box." They often feel less valued than younger employees who have contributed much less to the organization than they have. And they resent having to deal with these feelings after years of good service to the organization.

What comes across as belligerence and obstinacy is usually fear of failure and resentment over how they're being treated on this issue.

So, do you *lose* them anyway? And what do you *lose* if you do? You lose a ton of relationship management savvy—a commodity that's in very short supply these days, what with the negative baggage being in sales has acquired. You also may lose customers—a commodity that's in even shorter supply. You lose leadership and mentoring resources that are hard, if not impossible, to replace.

Now let's talk about the cost of keeping these resources. A confidential conversation to let them know that you understand their reluctance to use a computer, but that you need their leadership in implementing CRM, and you're going to help them get acclimated. A special class in running a computer, followed by another in Windows 98 or Windows 2000, both exclusively for non-computer users, preferably at an offsite location, led by an outside trainer who understands that the primary goal is having fun and creating a comfort level. A little patience and support, a little extra training, lots of encouragement, and understanding that becoming a computer user at an older age involves a lot of difficult feelings.

A very small price to pay to keep these resources, if you want to keep them. If you want to, you usually can. Not always, just as you can't always turn around a difficult situation with a younger employee. But most of the time.

Please recognize that you're asking more of older employees than their younger counterparts when you ask them to adopt CRM and work on computer. You'll have to work harder with them to help them through the transition. But what you get back repays you many times over for your efforts. If you sense sentiments from anywhere in your organization that CRM means ditching the "old folks," please try to turn that around.

Avoid E-Gregious Errors

E-mail marketing. It's gonna be big. It's gonna make us lots of moola. It's gonna expand the very horizons of database marketing. Right? Wrong. Wrong because what it's gonna do mostly is whiz off recipients to the point that they'll wire their e-mailboxes shut. And if they don't, their employers will.

Sure, relationship marketers will benefit from sending periodic e-mail messages to good customers. As long as the messages deliver perceived value to customers. If they don't and just shout "buy our stuff," they'll get stuffed. And don't fall into the "one purchase creates a customer relationship" nonsense. I once bought a book that Amazon.com didn't have from Barnes & Noble. Next time I'll use the library. My one book purchase has produced a torrent of Barnes & Noble e-mail that I could care less about—especially their ridiculous "Click Rewards" stuff that some frequency marketing sales person foisted off on B&N. This garbage even evades my Outlook junk mail filter. They're so clever that they've persuaded me never to go near Barnes & Noble anything again—except for bricks and mortar, and the bad taste in my mouth keeps me outta there pretty much.

Hey, let's use a little common sense. If we assign our tolerance for direct mail a value of 100, then our tolerance for telemarketing might be 1—and our tolerance for promotional e-mail is probably something like .000000001. My e-mail box is my e-mail box, and if you clutter it up you'll never see a nickel of my money. But you won't have the opportunity to bother me much longer. That's because there's an exciting new wave of technology on the way—much more powerful junk mail filters that shut you out after the first try, no matter how hard you try to disguise who you are. It's a race, I guess, between new filters and new legislation.

Let's Leave
The 'R' in CRM

Some marketers are saying it's the day of web-centric marketing. Others are saying it's the day of data-centric marketing. I don't know which day they're talking about, but it had to be a short one. Might do them a heap of good to open their eyes and discover it's the *era of customer-centric marketing.* You know, the "R" in CRM.

Of course, they have to *want* to open their eyes. Many don't. For many marketers, the thought of giving up their imagined control over customers is too much to bear—and too much to fear. "We can't let customers make their own decisions. We have to decide for them. Or they won't buy our products."

If that's truly the case, maybe they ought to improve their products. Try delivering value to customers instead of fluff and a gazillion *marketing messages.* But that would mean giving customers what *they* want, which might not be on the product roster *du jour.* "Hey, we've invested too much in what we sell to customers to let them decide they want otherwise."

So, instead of entering the new, customer-centric era, marketers are trying to force their old act into a new costume.

Wrap it up in web cloth and call it "new" and even "revolutionary." Stick it on the Internet and call it "inspiration." Call it "e-something.com." Who's going to know the difference?

Customers, that's who. The ones first patiently and now impatiently waiting for marketing to "get it." Sure the Internet is great, if you have what customers want. And if you do it their way. But that doesn't include more sleazy end-runs around people's privacy. Nor deaf marketers pushing out more promotional *talk*. Or putting direct marketing on the web and calling it new stuff. It's the same old stuff, and customers are sick of it.

What's really discouraging is to see so many use the web to *avoid* changing. Putting old worms in new cans. Deception— and ultimately, self-deception.

So look with jaundiced eyes and listen with jaundiced ears as the *e*-database marketers try to tell you they're doing something new by stuffing our e-mail boxes the same way they've stuffed our postal mail boxes. Or the *e*-service gurus hawk "self-service" as other than a naked attempt to cut service costs. Or the *e*-permission marketers stand on their soap boxes crowing, "They said we could. They said we could." Yeah, before they realized what they'd signed up for and now can't stop.

What do you think? Time to stop all this web hucksterism and go for real change—change that acknowledges the new primacy of customers? Better be time, because before long "www." is going to stand for "we were wrong." That, and customers are going to deal out some harsh lessons in what happens when you try to manage them, rather than work toward honest relationships.

Hey, I'm done now. Really. No more "one more things." Except to repeat myself, which I've probably done way too many times already, and wish you "good luck" on your way to CRM—and to steal the old *Hill Street Blues* television show line and say, "Hey, be careful out there."

VI. Other Stuff

Help!

With the CRM industry growing too fast to keep up with itself, you'd expect the available educational and support resources to be scant. And they are. That's the bad news. The good news is that the quality of what's out there is surprisingly high. Here's a short list of "go to" places that can help you keep your foot out of the proverbial bucket on your journey to CRM. In alphabetical order (for the protection of the author)...

- **Brendler Associates:** Head honcho Bill Brendler is a Ph.D. psychologist who applies his skills to helping companies through technology changes. He knows more about the organization issues set off by CRM than anyone I know. Make that more than any three people I know. When you see one of his journal articles, read it. If you're not seeing his journal articles, go up on his website and look at *www.brendler.com*.

- **CRMcommunity:** This lively site provides industry news, white papers, and even an "ask the consultant" feature that routes your questions to blokes like me. You won't want to ask me any more though, because I've already told you more than I know. Get there via *www.crmcommunity.com.*

- **CRMguru:** This even livelier site, hosted by FrontLine Solutions (see below), provides industry news, in-depth white papers, and an "ask the consultant" feature that routes your questions to blokes like me—then starts exchanges by subscribers on issues raised. You can even ask me questions, because you're likely to get multiple answers and lots of commentary. Don't miss this one. Go there today via *www.crmguru.com.*

- *Customer Relationship Management* **magazine (formerly *Sales & Marketing Automation,* formerly *Sales & Field Force Automation*):** As a colleague of mine recently introduced me to his client, "Dick is older than dirt." But as old as I am, I've never encountered a better trade publication in all my many years or working with 'em. Editor Larry Tuck gets it about CRM—and he's careful to include articles representing a broad range of perspectives— including mine. A *must read* for anyone serious about CRM. "And hey Larry, now do I get to do that article about marketing automation being a "Trojan horse" trying to co-opt CRM?" "What's that you're mumbling about 'death threats?'" Get this gem at *www.crmmag.com.*

  Same publisher does a companion called *Field Force Automation.* If you're heavy on the remote and wireless side check it out at *www.ffamag.com.* I don't write for them, so you're safe.

- **DCI:** DCI is the premier CRM trade show producer, hosting one a quarter in U.S. locations including Boston, Chicago, Los Angeles and New York—plus annual shows in London and Dusseldorf (what a "tax-subsidized vacation" temptation!). They frequently ask me to speak, which says a lot, and not that they're crazy, either. Good balance between educational sessions and exhibit hall stuff, but sessions tend to be light on strategy and heavy on technology—and a few too many turn into presenter commercials. They're currently trying to get a handle on the commercials, and who knows, they might well get the session content better aligned with what's happening in CRM.

  Get event schedules and content at *www.dci.com*. And if the content of one show doesn't grab you, check out the next. They change content frequently. Often enough to keep me current with PowerPoint.

- **Denali Group:** Rich Bohn, president of Denali Group who I mentioned last chapter, knows more about CRM technology than I've forgotten (which is saying a lot). Rich oozes street smarts, he's highly BS-resistant, and he has an aptly named website, *www.sellmorenow.com*. Check it out for all manner of CRM information including Rich's tell-it-like-it-is viewpoints. This guy is Andy Rooney in a sweater. Well, actually he's lots smarter. Especially about CRM software.

  Rich offers software selection consulting of the responsible kind. Considering the value of picking the optimal stuff, his services are a huge bargain. You can also purchase Denali Group's analyses of popular CRM software systems. Lots more accurate than investment research.

He also publishes a fantastic e-newsletter with lots of thoughtful commentary. Go up on his site and subscribe.

- **Front Line Solutions:** Bob Thompson, FLS's prez, does "partner relationship management" (PRM) stuff. Their site, which you can reach via *www.frontlinehq.com,* hosts streaming discussions and provides lots of valuable commentary on both PRM and CRM. If you sell through independent distribution, this site's a must. They also offer several excellent e-pubs—not just on PRM, but on CRM as well. Their subscription lists are growing like weeds, domestically and internationally. Don't get left out!

- **Information Week:** Think this pure propeller head stuff? Think again. The broader, what's-happening-in-business perspectives are first rate. And if you're not ready to tackle articles about XML (the knife that's gonna kill browser technology in CRM) and the like, definitely keep an eye peeled for articles by senior editor Jeff Sweat, who writes on front-office issues, and editor-in-chief Bob Evans, whose "Business/IT" column is at the back of every issue. Both are stellar. And hey, they absolutely don't let me write for them. Good sign. Go find it at *www.informationweek.com.*

- **Nurture Marketing:** You might call Jim Cecil, the proprietor, the conscience of database marketing. He's good at stuff like treating customers like people, rather than stick figures in a database with target images projected on their backs. He's become an icon in the customer-centricity movement—a status he richly deserves for relentlessly challenging the status quo in marketing. Check out Jim's thinking at *www.nurturemarketing.com.* Lots to learn up there. Very lots.

- **Peppers & Rogers Group:** These guys coined the "one-to-one" term (or is it "1:1" or "1 to 1?"). Whatever you call it, I call it "relationship marketing," which might be a bit wider umbrella if we want to split hairs. I don't, because I don't have any to spare, so let's not worry about branding customer-centric marketing. More importantly, they've done a great job communicating what customer-centric marketing is about. They publish lots of good stuff, some of it free, so make sure you visit them at *www.1to1.com.*

- **High-Yield Marketing:** If you burn this book after you read it, then decide you want to visit one of the aforementioned sites, you'll find links to almost all on our site *www.h-ym.com.* CRM educational material up there too. Wonder who's behind this veritable fountain of knowledge...?

About The Author

Richard A. (Dick) Lee
High-Yield Marketing

Dick Lee is principal of St. Paul, Minnesota-based High-Yield Marketing, a consulting group that helps clients develop CRM strategies and supporting systems. HYM emphasizes the strategic side of CRM—helping clients develop new customer relationship strategies, which drive new functional activities, which determine new work processes. With this foundation established, the firm then leads clients into deployment of appropriate CRM and front-office/back-office integration technologies.

Dick was among the founders of the relationship marketing movement, dating back to the early 1980s. Although he built a very successful advertising/direct marketing agency that he led until founding High-Yield Marketing in 1994, Dick's overriding interest has long been the melding of sales, marketing and technology into a powerful force for lengthening and strengthening customer relationships. While his clients have included 3M Company, American Express, Fidelity, General Electric,

Microsoft, Pitney-Bowes and Toro—his first love is working with middle market and small businesses that have the will and flexibility to become customer-driven organizations.

Dick, who is a popular public speaker, has written two category best-selling books—*The Sales Automation Survival Guide* and *The Customer Relationship Management Planning Guide*. He is currently working on the sequel to "Planning Guide," *The Customer Relationship Management Deployment Guide*. Dick's work and perspectives have been featured in *AdWeek, Customer Relationship Management, Sales & Field Force Automation, Sales & Marketing Automation, Potentials in Marketing,* National Public Radio's *MarketPlace* and *TheWall Street Journal.* His firm maintains a CRM education/resource website: *www.h-ym.com.*

Dick holds a BA from Reed College, Portland, Oregon, and an MBA from Suffolk University, Boston. Before devoting significant time to writing, Dick developed and taught at the Graduate School of Business, University of St. Thomas in Minneapolis, the first graduate-level business course in customer relationship marketing practices.

You are invited to forward comments about this book to Dick at *dlee@h-ym.com.*

About HYM's "Working Guide" Books

In 1999, HYM Press released *The Customer Relationship Management Planning Guide*, a "working guide" to help CRM adopting organizations develop customer-centric strategies. Although the planning regimen described had been considered proprietary and carefully protected in the past, frequent requests by attendees of Mr. Lee's workshops for resources to help guide them in making the transition to more customer-centric operations made a compelling case for releasing the methodology. Hence, the planning "checklist" employed by HYM with consulting projects was fleshed out with explanatory text to support unsupervised client use.

In a similar vein, we are now completing a companion working guide, *The Customer Relationship Management Deployment Guide*, designed to help clients overcome persistent problems with the process re-engineering and technology specification/selection aspects of implementing CRM. "Deployment Guide" is due for release during the summer of 2000.

Here is how CRM pundit Rich Bohn of Denali Group reviewed "Planning Guide."

World Famous SFA/CRM Guru Spills the Family Jewels

Most consultants guard their little tricks and methodologies like the priceless family jewels. So I was surprised to see Dick Lee's latest contribution to the genre, *The Customer Relationship Management Planning Guide*. In this slim publication, Lee spells out, in meticulous detail, the precise methodology he has used to guide numerous clients to successful CRM projects.

Many of you call me to discuss the challenges you are having getting your CRM project off the ground. Yet, just as many of you tell me you're not ready to pay a king's ransom to bring in a fancy consulting firm to lead you every step of the way. Well, you should look at Dick Lee's new guide. At just $175, this workbook will save you lots of time and energy. Get more details at Dick's website, *http://www.h-ym.com/*.

© 1999   Denali Group   *www.sellmorenow.com*

User comments are available in "Customer Reviews" on Amazon.com.